GODIVA'S HERITAGE:
COVENTRY'S INDUSTRY

by
Albert Smith & David Fry

SIMANDA PRESS
BERKSWELL 1997

GODIVA'S HERITAGE: COVENTRY'S INDUSTRY

CONTENTS

The compilers would welcome comments and further information. These may be addressed to:

Simanda Press
1 Meriden Road
Berkswell
Coventry CV7 7BE

INTRODUCTION

After producing the first two selections of 'The Coventry We Have Lost', ideas for a third were not long in arriving. Indeed since the mid 1990s so much re-development has been projected, especially for the centre of Coventry, it has been difficult to know where to draw the line. However, with many significant areas of change still to be finally decided we have postponed a third edition for another couple of years. Instead this book is more a reflection on the identity that Coventry has retained from its recent and not so recent past.

When Coventry is spoken of in positive terms what are those elements that characterise its image? Inevitably it will vary greatly from individual to individual and whether the person is a Coventrian or an outsider. The latter, if they know anything of Coventry at all will associate it with Lady Godiva. Those who are more knowledgeable will mention the car industry. Both are important aspects to Coventrians also, but for those who really know their Coventry will talk of the 'Coventry Kid'. The independent minded skilled worker whose expertise in many areas of industry, especially engineering, has made Coventry what it is today. Those skills were being honed in industries that existed long before the car industry came on the scene. Though often male, as will be seen, the role of female workers in Coventry's industrial heritage was also significant.

So Godiva and Industry are our two main themes. This book aims to illustrate these aspects of Coventry's heritage, as before, mainly by using photographic evidence that survives on old postcards. This time it seemed appropriate to make greater use of sources of evidence from various ephemera to support the photographs. For simplicity's sake the book concentrates mainly on sources that date from the first half of this century up to the Second World War. This is a time beyond the memory of many, but not sufficiently distant so that it fails to have a connection with the lives of people in the city today. As such we hope it will awaken half-remembered comments by older relatives and for current Coventrians reinforce knowledge and possibly pride in their city and its heritage.

We would like to take the opportunity to mention the many 'Coventry Kids' who are no longer with us who have made the twentieth century such an important one in Coventry's history and to dedicate this book to the likes of Sam Wright and his son Gilbert, Les Wainwright, Len Yates, Jack Brown and all the others who took a real interest in their city and spent their lives working in Coventry's industry.

THE GODIVA PROCESSIONS

Lady Godiva procession c1840 passing along Broadgate into High Street.

By far the most famous historical character associated with Coventry is that of Lady Godiva. She is a celebrity of whom Coventrians can feel justifiably proud. The symbolism of an individual's self sacrifice for the good of others has been the oft-quoted moral of the Godiva story. Doubts remain, however, as to how long her actions would have been celebrated if she had been set a less memorable though none the less humiliating task. The story of a Saxon countess riding naked through the streets of Coventry to save the townsfolk from the harsh taxation of her husband Earl Leofric has had a guaranteed popularity down the ages.

Many books have been written about Godiva, but little space is taken up with writing about her life because there is so little known. Godiva herself is definitely not a creation of legend though a few have grown up around her. We can be certain that she was alive in eleventh century England, married to Leofric, Earl of Mercia and that she died soon after the Norman Conquest. Her link with Coventry is quite clear. The Doomsday Book records her ownership of the settlement and she and Leofric are credited with founding a Benedictine monastery at Coventry, supposedly in 1043; this was also their final resting-place. As for the story of her ride through Coventry's streets, there is no contemporary evidence. The earliest written account was made almost two centuries after Godiva's death and the first mention of Peeping Tom was not made until the seventeenth century.

The point here is not to spoil a good story but to see how the Godiva story played a significant part in the life of Coventry until comparatively recently. The introduction of a procession with a rider representing Lady Godiva as its focus only came about as late as 1678, but then continued more or less annually until the mid nineteenth century. It usually coincided with the city's Great Whitsun Fair. These sorts of events often got out of hand because occasions for people to let off steam were still comparatively rare. But later the growth of Victorian prudery together with the robust celebration of Godiva's ride provided a convenient focus for blame by local religious leaders and the city fathers. Local traders did not help by circulating rumours before the event that *this* ride was to be a *totally* accurate representation of the original. Such speculation continued into this century's events spurred on by the money generating potential that those extra visitors would bring. There is no doubt that the commercial attraction of visitors who would at times double the city's population was a major factor in maintaining the procession in the face of disapproval from some quarters. None of the rumours ever proved to be true except on one occasion, in 1854, when a contemporary streaker on a horse gatecrashed the procession. This rival Godiva upstaged the (always) coyly covered official Godiva creating mayhem around the route. It was to be another eight years before another procession would be risked. The 1862 event was revived against vehement protests by various religious bodies despite assurances that Madam Letitia who was to depict Lady Godiva was unlikely to excite the crowds being *'fair, fat and forty'*. From that time until the Second World War only another fifteen or so processions of any significance were organised. Yet the greater rarity served to raise the profile of the occasion when it did occur and with the advent of photography was celebrated with appropriate souvenirs, even before the popular use of postcards in the twentieth century. Most nineteenth century photographs used here were produced as carte-de-visits, little bigger than a credit card. Photography was expensive and this size kept the costs down. These became available during the 1860s, but some of the later Godivas were also produced as cabinet photographs that were about three times as big.

Godiva processions have been just as infrequent since the Second World War. They certainly do not attract the crowds as they did in the past. Even the last pre-war procession of 1936 had around 200,000 people (300,000 by some accounts) lining the route. The free spectacle was still a great attraction in the age of the cinema, but even then was losing some of its popularity. The benefits of greater leisure time, a wider range of leisure activities and greater sophistication took the edge off the novelty of watching a re-enactment of the Lady Godiva legend. But the identification of Godiva with Coventry remains important to Coventrians as can be witnessed by the location of the 1949 statue right at the heart of the town as well as the use of Godiva as the City council logo. Furthermore frequent references to Godiva, in one form or another, in popular culture suggests she has an appeal far beyond the city. As such Godiva is an important part of Coventry's heritage and identity.

Most of the comments of the processions that follow have been taken from contemporary accounts, mainly newspapers. They were obviously written with some relish and no little humour. It seems that whilst the occasion itself was treated seriously and the historical personage of Lady Godiva was spoken of with due deference, her modern imitators were considered fair game for less respectful comments. The accounts of the selection of Godiva by committee, often of the more elderly and respectable males of the community, was frequently full of innuendo that would not have been out of place in a 'Carry On' film.

Miss Rose Williams, St Mary's Hall, Monday 20ᵗʰ June 1870 (Wingrave)

With four years since the last procession there was an eager anticipation for the depiction of Lady Godiva by Madam Stacey from the Royal Academy. The organisers became concerned when she had not turned up for the traditional overnight stay at St Mary's Hall so Rose Williams was selected at short notice as substitute. However, the situation developed into farce when Madame Stacey arrived an hour before the procession was to begin and insisted that she should take part. The organisers did not think that this was fair and as a result Madam Stacey subsequently took legal action to reclaim her expenses. Some confusion was caused because of the ruckus at the start, as Godiva was not in her advertised place in the procession. The procession itself seemed almost overshadowed by this drama as many felt that Rose Williams was not a convincing substitute. The crowds were still treated to the normal historical pageant. There was also the, by now, traditional elephant that had been first introduced in 1848 to represent the City Arms, albeit only a 16 month old baby. This time there was also a 'war camel' whose link with Coventry's past was rather more mysterious.

Miss Edgerton, St Mary's Hall, Monday 4ᵗʰ June 1877 (Wingrave)

Yet another controversial procession was arranged at a few months notice in 1877. Initially there was support from a number of official quarters but in the end the event was carried by the commercial interests in the city. The local garrison refused escorts of soldiers, however, yeomanry were promised by Lord Aylesford but then withdrawn by Earl Warwick. Eventually an event was cobbled together and a Godiva engaged from Sangster's & Astley's Amphitheatre, London. The dress was described as *not 'indecent'* and *'a good deal less objectionable than the costume of 1870'*. To judge from the photographs there was not much in it. Miss Edgerton wore silk salmon tights, white satin bodice and trunks, trimmed with silver lace and covered by a semi-transparent veil. Throughout the four-and-a-half hours of the procession she was met with approving cheers by all along the route, which could not be said of all representatives of Godiva in the past. One sour note was sounded by the Daily Express reporter who sarcastically praised the way that Godiva had again helped the needy tradesmen of the city as she had done with her original ride. In the same flippant state of mind he went on to suggest that Godiva should ride on a bicycle in tribute to the way that industry had saved the city from the ribbon trade depression.

Maude Forester, Bayley Lane, Monday 6th August 1883 (George Dew)

The large cabinet photograph, shown above hides the rather substantial figure of London's Maude Forester, harking back perhaps to the 1862 rational of keeping the crowds calm with a less alluring Godiva than a slimmer personification. This created a few problems as her saddle was too small and she broke the stirrup on mounting the horse. Maude Forester does, however, share with previous and subsequent Godivas the standard costume of long hair and 'fleshings' (the latter being a form of body stocking ensuring no naked flesh would be exposed). The 1883 procession was the first to be held in August instead of the traditional Whitsun, in the hope of better weather. Certainly the crowds flocked to Coventry in large numbers, especially by rail, at least ten thousand from Birmingham, let alone several thousand from surrounding towns. It is not too surprising that this event should be so well attended for not only was it a free spectacle but had also been the subject of national debate. A letter to The Times the previous week had described the procession as *'a stupendous and vulgar piece of tomfoolery'*. The citizens of Coventry were not to be put off and to judge from an account in The Coventry Herald the event was viewed more a pantomime than a solemn occasion.

It is worth noting that all formal photographs and paintings of the various Lady Godivas have nearly always been set in the precincts of St Mary's Hall in Bailey Lane, as these two here have been. Despite being built almost three centuries after Godiva's death, St Mary's has developed a close association with the Godiva story.

1907 LADY GODIVA, LA MILO (MISS PANSY MONTAGUE)

La Milo (Miss Pansy Montague), Wednesday 7th August 1907 (J J Ward)

The 1907 procession was the second major Godiva procession of the twentieth century, following five years after the coronation procession of 1902. Although at the time the idea of pageants had caught on in many other towns, the Coventry procession was still the only one of any size that was free to the public and not restricted to showgrounds. As ever the presence of a woman portraying Godiva's ride attracted national interest and the nature of her clothing provoked great controversy. As in 1883 various clerics and ministers had stirred up a storm of controversy commenting on the vulgarity of the proceedings. This prompted La Milo, otherwise known as Pansy Montague, to issue a long statement on the night before her ride, defending her position. She described her critics as *'narrow minded, bigoted, misguided'* and their comments were *'an outrage on the common sense and high intentions of those responsible for the arrangements of the procession.'* Also that by their actions they had *'jeopardised the prospect of raising a large sum of money for an urgent charitable purpose'*. The charitable purpose was to raise money for the Coventry Hospital – a target of a £1000 had been set. As it turned out the day went well and even the traditional rain held off. La Milo was selected from a large number of applicants and once chosen offered her services for free as the event was in aid of charity. She was apparently a leading exponent of the art of 'living statuary', displaying what was considered to be 'the most perfect of feminine figures' on the English stage. She was 21 years old 5ft 8in tall, a skilled equestrienne and fond of motoring. La Milo stayed in Coventry overnight at St Mary's Hall, as many Godivas had before.

Elephant, Cox Street, 1907 (Unknown)

This living incarnation of the City's Coat of Arms was a mixed success, the tower was considered realistic by reporters but the figure on a wire structure above it was something of a mystery. The elephant was a great surprise to people on the journey, as it did not feature in the programme being thought to be impossible to bring to the city in time. Before entering the Butts it needed to get a quick drink from the Sherbourne. The picture shows the procession having just turned into Cox Street from Ford Street with the Sydenham Palace above the elephant and the Sevengraph Works of Thomas Stevens in the right foreground.

Humber Silver Band, Cox Street 1907 (Unknown)

This view is from close to the front of the procession and the last of the mounted police that led the way can just be seen on the left. The photograph was taken soon after the procession had begun, the participants having travelled out of Pool Meadow and along Ford Street and almost to the top of Cox Street, ready to turn into Jordan Well. The pub on the left is the Robin Hood Inn. Behind the Humber Silver Band and to the left of the horse drawn fire engine is the entrance to New Street.

La Milo, Fleet Street/Smithford Street 1907 (Unknown)

Although the many visitors to the city brought extra trade quite a few shops would close and barricade their windows from the crush., however, the proprietor of the Co-op in Fleet Street was clearly being over protective. In the previous century there would have been quite a lot of theatrical activity *in* this building it being the old Britannia Music Hall. The procession is moving down Smithford Street into Fleet Street. La Milo had her sister Muriel travelled in a carriage behind the canopy to offer moral support.

La Milo, Spon Street 1907 (Unknown)

The procession had gathered at Pool Meadow as the largest open area in the centre of the town and the public baths there were used for changing. The journey was to take five hours to cover six miles and the procession itself was two miles in length. They left Pool Meadow soon after being joined by La Milo who had ridden down from her overnight stay at St Mary's Hall. The clock outside Bird's Chemist shows that it was five past one at that point in the journey, less than an hour after the first people left Pool Meadow. The procession is heading out of town toward Spon End where today the inner edge of the Ring Road cuts across Spon Street.

La Milo, Spon End 1907 (Unknown)

The procession has reached the stage where La Milo was about to turn out of Spon Street into the Butts at Spon End. Behind can be seen the Chapel of St James and St Christopher by Spon Bridge (See page 13 *TCWHL Vol 1*). Although not having being used as a chapel for a few hundred years it represents one of the oldest buildings along the traditional Godiva route, but even so Godiva had been dead for three hundred years when its foundations were laid.

The Fire Brigade, The Butts 1907 (Unknown)

Here Coventry's Fire Brigade can be seen at the front of the procession at this point. Their horse drawn fire engine is steam powered and appropriately named 'Peeping Tom'. The firemen are led by Captain Armishaw who is standing to the right of the driver Just behind is one of the trade floats showing the work of Alfred Herbert Ltd. The newspapers commented on the hundreds of sightseers with their binoculars and cameras, many climbing onto walls and roofs. The houses on the right are by the junction of the Butts with Thomas Street. The trees opposite are in the grounds of St Thomas's church at the bottom of Albany Road.

Ancient Druids, The Butts 1907 (Edwards & Co)

At some places along the route large stands were erected for the comfort of spectators. A rather smaller one was made outside the factory of machine tool manufacturer Alfred Herbert, shown here. As can also be seen the Druids have attempted to construct a mini Stonehenge on their float with the brothers and officers of the order dressed in full regalia. The view shows the south side of Queens Road opposite the entrance to Hertford Place. Alfred Herbert moved out of the factory in 1930 and part of the factory was used as an abattoir. Much later it became an extension of the Technical College (See page 79).

La Milo, Broadgate 1907 (Harvey Barton)

The city was remarkably full as this view of Broadgate testifies. As many as 150,00 people were estimated to be on the streets and the railways had made arrangement to carry at least 25,000 visitors. Americans visitors had been noted at previous processions but in 1907 were present in large numbers. Despite the obvious density of the crowd, which remained packed for most of the day, the lack of any marshals was a tribute to the discipline of the spectators. But there were extra police out on the streets and 20 incidents of pick pocketing were recorded.

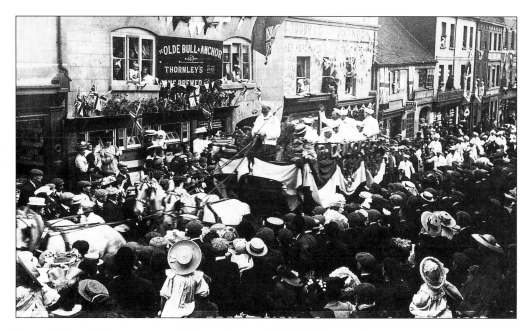

Coventry Master Bakers' Association, Bishop Street 1907 (Unknown)

The Master Bakers float with their eight outriders behind were one of the few shop trades represented in the procession. Their float was covered with varieties of loaf and even the lettering on the side was made of bread. The procession is now half way up Bishop Street on its way to the Foleshill Road. Pubs like the Olde Bull and Anchor did a roaring trade and despite one pub having already sold out of beer by one o'clock there was little reported drunkenness.

La Milo, White Street 1907 (Unknown)

The procession is shown turning out of Bird Street into White Street with Swanswell Pool and St Mark's church to the right. La Milo is doing well to maintain a fixed smile four hours into the journey. The Coventry Herald reported the passing of Godiva thus: *'children were hoisted shoulder high, and the crowd narrowed the path shouting." She's coming." etc. Cheers, loud and sustained greeted her and she smilingly acknowledged the ovation; then came comment, entirely of approval. Exclamations of delight were heard on all sides. "how beautiful" and "how lovely she looks," and the question "What can there be to object to?" came from many lips'.*

La Milo, Much Park Street 1907 (Unknown)
Daimler Renard Train, Much Park Street 1907 (Unknown)

La Milo had entered Much Park Street from the London Road end. The first view was taken just a small distance east of Short Street, now under the Ring Road. The second view is nearer town showing the old gatehouse entrance to Whitefriars Lane (The old toy museum) just behind the second carriage of the train with the Rose Inn beside flying a large flag. Note La Milo's wig that was a matter of some controversy being golden brown rather than the traditional blond of Godiva and also rather too substantial for the likes of the spectators. The canopy was constantly on hand in case of rain which featured more frequently in Godiva processions than not. In 1907 an old tradition was revived from the medieval period of having a trades section to the procession. Daimler made a particular impression with their 'road train'. Rather impractical for British roads it was made under licence from the French firm Renard who had developed it.

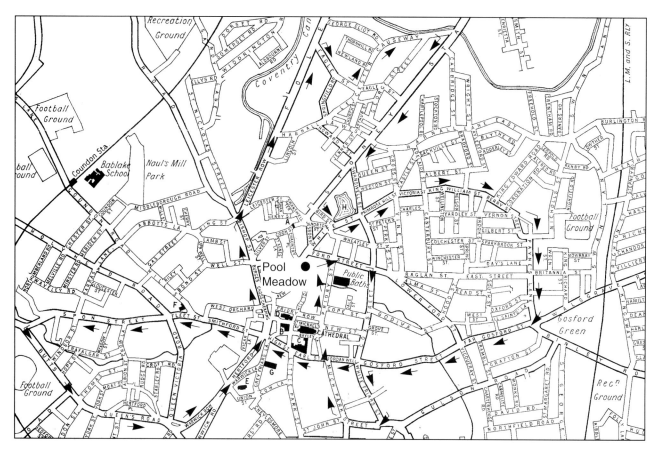

These two maps show the routes taken by the 1907 and 1911 Godiva processions. The 1907 shown above started from Pool Meadow and took a mainly clockwise route around the City, whereas the 1911 shown below, started from Barrack Square and went mainly anti-clockwise. Although the 1911 event was slightly less in distance it was still 5 miles and took nearly three and half-hours to complete.

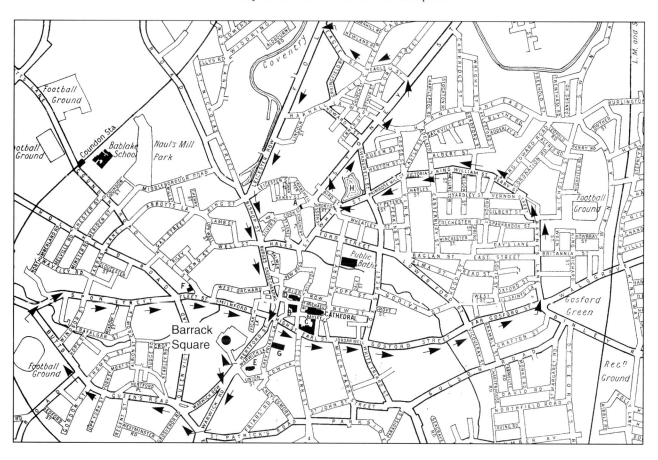

1911 LADY GODIVA, MISS VIOLA HAMILTON

Miss Viola Hamilton, St Mary's Hall, Thursday 22nd June 1911 (Maule & Co)

The 1911 event was organised to be part of Coventry's celebration of the coronation of King George V. The local paper noted that the public were more *'gone on'* pageantry than ever before. A London actress was hired as Lady Godiva and events were reportedly organised in a much more efficient way than before. However, it is difficult to avoid the impression from reading the contemporary press accounts that there was not quite the same enthusiasm as the 1907 event. For one thing there was nothing like the same controversy as accompanied previous processions with regard to Godiva's manner of dress. After the quite tame appearance of La Milo, thanks to the all-consuming wig it was thought that Viola Hamilton would be equally discreet. But to judge from her studio photographs when stripped down to her 'fleshings' Miss Hamilton left less to the imagination. Unlike La Milo she was fortunate enough to possess her own traditional flaxen coloured hair, but though very long it needed lengthening and thickening a little with extensions. Most reports agreed that this Godiva was the best for at least half a century. Nevertheless, though the crowds were as numerous in parts of the city centre as for any previous procession, the suburbs were said to be quite quiet. Some figures support this; only 10,000 people arrived by train, less people cycled to the city as fewer people made money by storing the bikes safely for the day. It appeared that the procession itself was better than before, but with a windy and showery day in the offing and most other towns putting on their own celebrations, for once Coventry relied more on its own citizens to fill the streets and the collections for the hospital fund. Viola Hamilton was to resurface thirty years later when she visited the London studio of sculptor Sir William Reid Dick who was engaged in modelling the Godiva statue that was to eventually stand in the re-built Broadgate in 1949.

Viola Hamilton, Warwick Road 1911 (Waterman)

In 1911 the procession gathered in the Barracks Square behind Hertford Street rather than Pool Meadow. At the point shown here the nineteen-year-old, 5 foot 8 inch Lady Godiva has just begun her journey, exiting the Barracks Square via Bull Yard into Warwick Road. To the left can be seen the Rover showrooms followed by the Reform Club and the railings at the entrance to Greyfriars Green. The route was a little less arduous than the 1907 procession having only five miles to cover.

Viola Hamilton, Warwick Road 1911 (Harvey Barton)

Just a few hundred yards further on from the previous photograph the procession is turning from Warwick Road into Queens Road by Stoneleigh Terrace. The large houses in the background were demolished when the Ring Road was built. The crowds had already seen 130 characters and bands before they got to see Viola Hamilton. She was considered to be the best looking representation of Godiva to be seen for a long time. She wore pink fleshings covered with gauze that was considered sufficiently discreet not to require the mass of coyly draped hair that La Milo was criticised for.

Viola Hamilton, Queens Road 1911 (Unknown)

A little further along Queens Road, the Baptist church can be seen in the background and Regent Road on the right. To the front is the carriage carrying the City Officials: Sword Bearer, Mace Bearer, City Chamberlain. This continued a tradition dating back to the earliest days of the procession revived in 1907. For the first time for years there was no husband for the leading lady as Earl Leofric's representative had unaccountably not turned up.

Viola Hamilton, Butts 1911 (Unknown)

This photograph is taken about two hundred metres along from the previous view, approaching the junction with Thomas Street. The distinctive watchmakers windows of J Newsome & Co can be seen in the background (See page 39). The gentleman with the boater accompanied Lady Godiva throughout the procession in case of problems with her horse, though, having learnt to ride with Buffalo Bill's Wild West Show she was thought a competent horsewoman.

Renard Road Train, Smithford Street 1911 (Waterman)
George IV and Escort of Warwickshire Gentry, High Street, 1911 (Unknown)

The Renard road train had first made an appearance in the 1907 procession, but this one, again constructed by the Daimler Motor Company, was bigger and more powerful. It weighed 30 tons and was pulled by an engine unit developing 80 HP. There were four trailers three depicted men at work on the different stages of constructing a motor car whilst the last showed a automatic turning machine used in car production and provided by Alfred Herbert. The progress of the train through the narrow streets of Coventry was greatly assisted by the ability of each trailer to be steered independently of the main unit. The lack of this facility had caused great problems for the 1907 road train. This view was taken at the top of Smithford Street ready to cross Broadgate into High Street. It is the work of the same photographer who took the picture near the start at Hertford Street, but like others had negotiated more than one viewing point. The second view shows the procession having just crossed over Broadgate and entering High Street. The historical content of the procession was particularly large even by the standards of previous processions. George IV's appearance was near the head of the procession accompanied by the city guards with their pikestaffs together with a few heralds in front of them. Behind the king is the escort of anonymous Warwickshire Gentry. The procession still has two thirds of its journey to go.

Salvation Army Band, King William Street 1911 (Unknown)

The two themes of the book meet here in Hillfields. The traditional industry of silk weaving centred in this district is evidenced by the series of large top shop windows in the tall buildings of King William Street, and the celebration of the Godiva story with its procession that was routed through Hillfields from soon after it was built. The view shows the north side of the street by the junction with Adelaide Street.

Viola Hamilton, Victoria Street 1911 (Unknown)

This view of the procession away from the city centre seems to contradict the report in the local paper that the streets of Hillfields *'were but thinly populated'*. Certainly this stretch of Victoria Street from the Crown Hotel at the top seems to be quite full. The inspiration of a nineteenth century French painting resulted in Godiva being led by nuns for the first time. Could this pious example explain the lack of reported pick pocketing in the 1911 event?

Mary Queen of Scots, Victoria Street/Primrose Hill Street 1911 (Harvey Barton)

Where Victoria Street runs into Primrose Hill Street, as today, stands the Royal Exchange though no longer as a pub. Various royal and noble personalities are represented here, the historical pageant being as dominant as ever in the 1911 event. Sadly the trade section was not really developed beyond the numbers seen in 1907.

Ancient Druids, Cross Cheaping 1911 (Harvey Barton)

The procession has only the length of Broadgate and Hertford Street to go. The Druids shown here had enjoyed a comfortable carriage ride surrounded by their boughs of mystical greenery. They are shown opposite the Talbot Inn by the entrance to West Orchard. This joyful scene in 1911 was to be replaced after the 1919 procession with one of rioting and damage, as can be clearly seen in the following section.

1919 LADY GODIVA, MISS GLADYS MANN

Miss Gladys Mann,
Saturday 19th July 1919,
(HH Thompson)

The 1919 pageant was something of a sorry affair, surprisingly so given the event it was supposed to be celebrating. This was the day laid down by the government to formally mark the signing of the Peace Treaty at Versailles exactly three weeks earlier. But the real celebrating had occurred eight months earlier on Armistice Day, when the spontaneous joy that the war was over was seen on the streets of Coventry. By July 1919 many soldiers had been discharged and the local press reported an atmosphere of quiet reflection rather than noisy scenes of earlier processions. However, the latent emotions that the day stirred up showed themselves over the next few nights when there was serious rioting and damage throughout the city centre. Other factors did not help the success of the day. As so often before the weather was not good with showers in the morning and a downpour in the afternoon. The procession itself was much shorter stressing the historical part of the procession, central to past occasions, but additional displays put on to celebrate local industry was thought inappropriate; a rather poor thanks for the vital role Coventry industry played in the war effort. As well as complaints that the procession was too short, the few that took part set such a cracking pace that those on foot had to trot at times to keep up, and those watching did not have enough time to work out who was supposed to be representing who! Early on (before the rain) the procession took just eleven minutes to pass, quite a contrast with the two-mile long procession of 1907. There were some positive aspects to the day. In the morning 15,000 Coventry school children took part in their own procession and one paper rather pointedly suggested that it might have been thought by many to be the feature of the day. Also Lady Godiva herself was for the first time in recent memory a Coventry woman, the daughter of a local councillor. She was an actress and though using her married name, in the style of the theatre, called herself Miss. A novel departure with tradition saw Godiva dressed in what was considered full Saxon court dress together with a spiked coronet. With such an outfit she was able to wear her longhaired wig in non-traditional plaits. The press considered this as preferable to 'gaudy pink fleshing and gauze that has marked most of the processions'. It might explain why this time the Bishop and a number of his clergy felt able to join the procession at the Council House, together with the Mayor, the local MP, councillors and the Earl of Craven. For the crowds, though, it was yet another reason for criticising the procession.

Broadgate/Cross Cheaping, Peace Riots 1919 (Unknown)
Cross Cheaping, Peace Riots 1919 (Unknown)

Many reasons have been given for the riots but none are conclusive. Whatever the case the basic facts are clear. Soon after 11.30pm, a few hours after the procession finished, a mob attacked Dunn's shoe shop in Broadgate whereupon a hundred police were quickly mobilised to deal with them. Thirty-five premises, mainly in Broadgate, Cross Cheaping, and Bishop Street areas had windows broken and looted. 64 people were treated in hospital. The top picture shows the worst affected area covering Broadgate and Cross Cheaping. Judging by the lack of traffic and the clock it was probably taken on the Sunday morning. The second view, looking up from Cross Cheaping shows the Talbot Inn suspiciously free from damage. This confirms that the photograph was taken on a Sunday, as it was to suffer in the final night of rioting on Monday. England's damaged shoe shop a little further up showed initiative with the amusing temporary notice *'ENGLAND BOMBARDED BUT THERE IS NO BETTER 'OLE THAN THIS IF YOU WANT THE GOODS'.*

1929 LADY GODIVA, MISS MURIEL MELLERUP

*Miss Muriel Mellerup,
St Mary's Hall,
Saturday 29th June 1929,
(Appleby)*

The photographs of the 1929 Godiva seem to be of a woman in some discomfort as if rather unhappy with her lot, but contemporary accounts reveal quite a different explanation. Apparently Miss Muriel Mellerup was attempting a faithful historical interpretation of her role, trying to give an impression of a dignified and graceful Lady Godiva with her eyes demurely downcast. Certainly in most other respects the procession was a success in the tradition of the very best of previous events. Unusually the weather was sunny for the occasion, but the first Godiva ride for a decade had stirred up an enthusiasm, it was claimed, that would not have been put off by bad weather anyway. The crowds were greater than ever with twenty special trains and up to 400 special buses bringing people into the city on the day, filling the streets to the extent that several people fainted. Visitors had already been arriving for a few days previously and all possible accommodation was taken. The first arrival of large numbers of Americans since the 1907 event was noted. There were at least forty in just one party at the Kings Head Hotel. The stimulus for the procession had come from a familiar source, the need to raise money to cover the increased costs of hospital building and care in Coventry. For the first time a static pageant in the recently opened Memorial Park was planned at the end of the procession through the streets. For this purpose a display area was created to seat 2000 paying spectators. However, this was the only addition to the otherwise traditional programme for the day as the route taken by Miss Mellerup was much the same as that travelled by other twentieth century Godivas. Even her appearance was a return to the traditional 'fleshings' after the cover-up by the previous Godiva. Sadly though it was also a return to a non-Coventrian as this Godiva returned on the Sunday to her home in Dursley, Gloucestershire.

Miss Muriel Mellerup, The Grove, Kenilworth Road 1929 (J J Ward)

By the inter-war years the use of postcards for mass communication had become much less popular. Most postcards for the three main processions of this period, 1919, 1929 and 1936 were simply studio based or statically posed shots. Commercially produced action shots of the actual processions are quite rare. This one was taken soon after three o'clock as the procession had only just left the entrance of Memorial Park, passing by the junction with Leamington Road.

Hospital patients awaiting the procession, 1929 (Unknown)

Since 1907 the person playing Lady Godiva would stop at the Coventry and Warwickshire hospital and visit the patients. This was considered one of the main highlights of the day but was rarely captured on camera. A terrace of 160 beds had been arranged at the end of Bird Street.

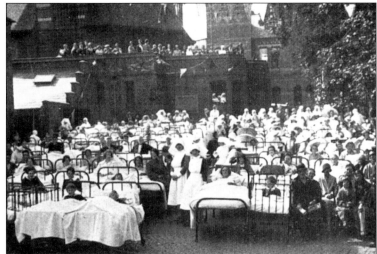

Miss Mellerup, Russell Arms, The Butts 1929 (Unknown)

The landlord of the Russell Arms distributed this small photograph with his name proudly printed on the back. The pub was opposite Broomfield Place in the Butts and was at an early stage in the route as the traditional tour of Foleshill, Hillfields and the town centre was yet to come.

The Procession, 1936

ROUTE OF PROCESSION

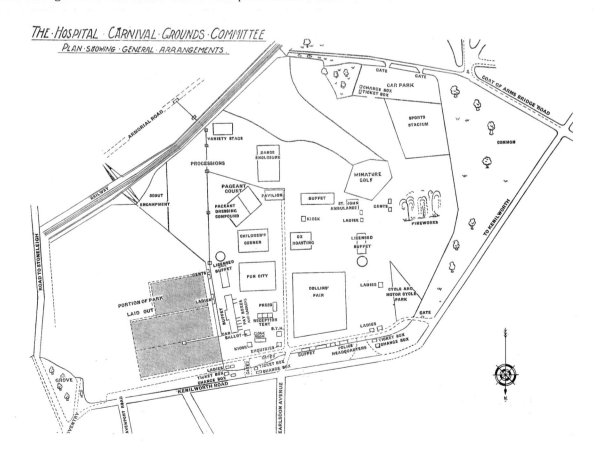

SPON END SPON ST.

CORPORATION ST.

BISHOP ST.

FOLESHILL RD.

EAGLE ST.

BUTTS

1929 ROUTE

SMITHFORD ST.

CROSS CHEAPING BURGES

10 MIN. STOP, HOSPITAL

BIRD ST.

STONEY STANTON RD.

QUEENS RD.

BROADGATE

PRIMROSE HILL ST.

KING WILLIAM ST.

KENILWORTH RD.

WARWICK RD.

HERTFORD ST.

HIGH ST. EARL ST.

COUNCIL HOUSE

PAYNES LANE

START 3. P.M.

MEMORIAL PARK

L.M.S STATION.

JORDAN WELL GOSFORD ST.

GOSFORD GREEN 5 MIN. STOP.

Chief Marshal:
F. W. Swinnerton.

THE PROCESSION starts at 3 p.m. from the MEMORIAL PARK.

Both the 1929 and 1936 Godiva processions started from the Memorial Park, the routes being much shorter than previous events. The 1936 event was slightly different from the 1929 route as by 1936 Corporation Street had been opened. From Spon Street, Corporation Street to Bishop Street was used rather than Smithford Street, Cross Cheaping and The Burges. The view above is of the 1936 route. The view below gives some idea of the arrangements and events due to take place at the Park.

1936 LADY GODIVA, MISS FRANCES P BURCHELL

*Miss Frances P Burchell,
St Mary's Hall, Saturday
27th June 1936,
(Clayton)*

This was to be the last great Godiva procession celebrated before the public became more blasé about their pleasures, seduced by television and the technicolor cinema. Nevertheless twentieth century technology was still having an impact on this occasion also. The Coventry Herald, unused to the presence of microphones and loudspeakers headlined its report 'MICROPHONES AT THE MEMORIAL PARK', later commenting that '*So often were voices heard booming through loudspeakers that there seemed to be something amiss when the announcers were pausing for breath simultaneously at the mikes*'. The assembly of attractions at Memorial Park developed a dimension to the day that was first seen at the 1929 event. Many stayed to

enjoy the events for the rest of the day even after the procession had departed. The highlight of the evening came at 11 o'clock when 50,000 people enjoyed a firework display.

The procession had begun in the park eight hours earlier, parading in a temporary stadium in front of a crowd who had paid between 2s 6d and 5s to have a comfortable preview of the entrants. As the procession took an hour to pass any one point on its six-mile route, a seat in the stands was worth the expense to many. But the entrance money together with the thousands of pounds collected along the route was freely given in support of the Coventry Hospital Fund. Miss Burchell from Harbourne, Birmingham led the procession that was even more appropriately themed than normal. Instead of famous characters from Coventry's history representation was made of famous female characters; an approach to historical analysis that was ahead of its time. The theme found approval with the mayor who thought '*The tone of the whole procession is indeed of a high standard*'.

Miss Frances P Burchell, Memorial Park 1936 (Unknown)

A competent amateur who clearly had privileged access at the Memorial Park took this picture. The photograph shows how much more daring the Godiva costume had come. This time only a close fitting body stocking without the other items of clothing or unnaturally thick wigs of previous incumbents. The Mayor can be seen by the horse ready to see Miss Burchell off on her ride. He was also at hand when the procession reached the City hospital to drape a cloak over her shoulders as she dismounted to meet the patients.

Stevengraph of 1840s Lady Godiva Procession, Broadgate *c 1905*

A number of postcards were produced in the early years of this century featuring woven silk inserts of various scenes. Most of these were the product of Thomas Stevens of Cox Street who in 1862 first sold the fruits of his invention for producing complex silk pictures and designs on Jacquard looms. This postcard features a silk copy of an engraving of a Victorian Godiva procession made in the first half of the nineteenth century (see page 4) and acts as an appropriate link to the other significant facet that goes to make up Coventry's heritage; its industry.

INDUSTRY

It is difficult to find another British town that experienced a similar transformation of industrial fortunes in such a short time as Coventry did. Most industrial centres were well established by the time that Coventry began to develop its full economic muscle.

Early in the last century it looked as if Coventry's position as the main producer of silk ribbons in the country would assure a degree of prosperity into the future, but it was not to be. Like the car industry in the second half of the twentieth century, Coventry was too dependent on one industry and once that got into difficulty it was really in trouble. So while the rest of the country saw economic expansion, in the early 1860s a third of the city's inhabitants were dependent on hand outs from soup kitchens. A tenth of the population left the city during these years. The city's other major industry, watch-making, fared little better as the century ended, though it did employ only a quarter as many people. But by 1880 salvation was at hand in the form of the emerging cycle industry. It was attracted by the coincidence of a pool of skilled, unemployed labour, the talent of local entrepreneurs and inventors and a location in the centre of the country. This in turn attracted similar new high-tech industry of the time to make use of the ready supply of trained labour and appropriate support industry. Such a virtuous circle of prosperity was to see Coventry's population grow by 50% in the first decade of the twentieth century, far outstripping the growth of other industrial towns. The recently established car industry was by now moving out of its 'anyone can have a go' experimental stage and was starting to be dominated by a handful of big players. Associated machine tool and electrical industries were being attracted by the demand for motor parts. Coincidentally the city became famous again for textiles as the location of Courtaulds's new artificial fibre factory. As if the momentum of these changes were not enough to secure Coventry's future prosperity the demands of the 1914-18 War were to stretch its productive capacity to the limit. Despite the economic depressions that followed in the inter-war period, Coventry prospered more than most on the back of its wartime investments. Again in the 1930s the prospect of war brought new investment to the city. Whilst the destruction by the German bombers was of significant social note it did little to slow Coventry's Industrial progress. The post war boom meant that the success story continued through the 1950s and 1960s only for the shocks of the 1970s and 1980s to be felt more profoundly than at any time in the previous century of economic growth.

For anyone living through the last few decades the gradual haul out of this recent period of economic decline seemed painfully slow, but the construction sites across the city and the attraction of many firms to new and old industrial areas give cause for optimism. There maybe some regrets that few fit into the Coventry tradition of manufacturing industry, but this is no more than part of a national trend where the workforce is moving into the provision of services rather than goods.

1. Finished Lathes in the Erecting Department of Messrs. Alfred Herbert Limited.

2. The largest hammer in the world, with an anvil Block of forged steel weighing 146 tons, at Messrs. Brett's Patent Lifter Company Limited.

3. The Winding Department of the British Thomson-Houston Company's Coventry Works.

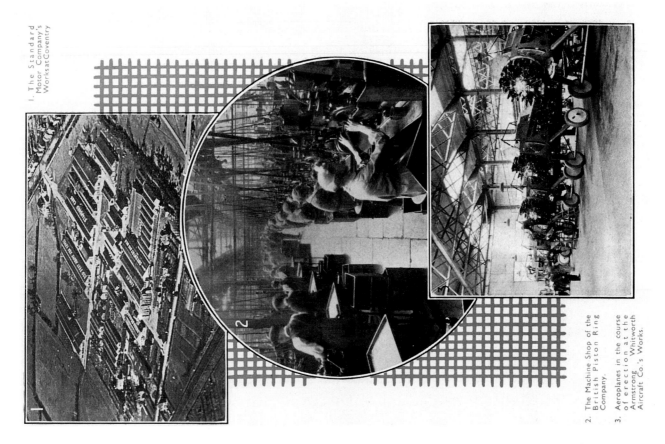

1. The Standard Motor Company's Works at Coventry.

2. The Machine Shop of the British Piston Ring Company.

3. Aeroplanes in the course of erection at the Armstrong Whitworth Aircraft Co.'s Works.

These two pages taken from a mid 1930's booklet listing Coventry industry give a good indication of the number of activities carried on in the city. Later in the booklet it lists over 180 different products made.

1. A Coventry Motor Car Erecting Shop.

2. Wire Wheel Building at The Coventry Factory of The Dunlop Rim and Wheel Company.

3. The Daimler Company's 'Bus Erecting Shop.

4. Heavy Battery of Hammers in operation at The Albion Drop Forgings Company Limited.

5. The Radio Test Section of the General Electric Company Limited.

6. The manufacture of woven names at Messrs. J. & J. Cash Limited.

TEXTILES

Coventry's medieval wealth was based on its control of the local wool trade and associated textile trades. Despite the rapid decline of the industry after the dissolution of the monasteries it was still of some significance well into the 1700s. But by this time silk weaving had taken over as the principal textile industry although the details of its development remain rather mysterious. By the nineteenth century silk weaving was carried out throughout Coventry and surrounding villages. They worked in a very specialised market producing only narrow bands of fancy designs – ribbons for the fashion market. As such they were susceptible to the vagaries of fashion. Production was chiefly a cottage industry based in the home. The use of steam powered factories was not popular. But by the middle of the century a peculiar Coventry version of the Industrial Revolution had been worked out whereby people could still work in their own homes. Houses would be grouped so that steam power could be provided as required to power their individual looms kept in the 'the shop on the second or third floor. The Cash brothers built one of the largest versions of this system that still survives at Cash's Lane. Inevitably, perhaps, such adaptations to the demands of industrial change were not sufficient to save the industry. It was decimated in the 1860s and more than half the workers were lost in just a few years. Leigh Mills in Hill Street was opened in 1863 to offer employment to weavers, but this factory was only concerned with woollen goods. Just a few silk weaving businesses like Cash's specialising in various forms of silk weaving such as clothes labelling and Stevens making silk pictures and bookmarks survived well into this century. Though many other small businesses dealing in fine textile work survived well into the century it was the opening of Courtaulds's factory in 1904 that was to be the new champion of Coventry's textile heritage.

The Late Harry Laxton and his working model of a silk ribbon weaving frame c1910 (JT Hall)

Because of the decline of ribbon weaving before the end of the last century pictures of looms on postcards are rare. This is therefore an unusual illustration of a loom constructed as a tribute to the industry. The shaft and wheel where a steam driven pulley would be attached can be seen at the rear of the loom. Up to twenty ribbons could be woven at once on some of these looms. There is no note of a Harry Laxton at this period in Coventry though a number of people with that surname were living there. It is possible that this Harry Laxton was the William H Laxton who was a picture framemaker in 1912 at 76 Much Park Street as this was an important district for ribbon weaving throughout its survival in Coventry.

J&J Cash, Cash's Lane c1912 (Unknown)
Cash's Trimmings, c1910 (Unknown)

When built in 1857 the Cash brothers project seemed to offer a way forward for an otherwise doomed industry. Coventry silk weavers were facing competition from abroad despite strong protective tariffs and the Kingfield cottage factory, Cash's Lane, Foleshill, seemed to offer the best way of meeting this competition. The weavers were able to have their traditional independence by living and working at home but the top floor of their houses would be like a large factory. Sixteen of those houses are shown here, fronting the later factory, part of an original scheme for 100. Before it could be completed the protective tariffs had been taken and a more conventional factory production technique was adopted. Part of the adjustment to a new competitive environment was to move into areas apart from silk ribbons, but that still needed the delicate weaving skill that was part of the Coventry tradition. Most commonly this has been perceived to be silk pictures and bookmarks, but to the right can be seen an early twentieth century advertising postcard depicting a less well known product – frilly trimmings for dolls clothes!

THERE IS NOTHING LIKE CASH'S FRILLINGS FOR TRIMMING CHILDREN'S AND INFANTS' WASHING GARMENTS"

PATTERN BOOK WILL BE SENT TO ANY ADDRESS ON APPLICATION TO J. & J. CASH LTD. COVENTRY

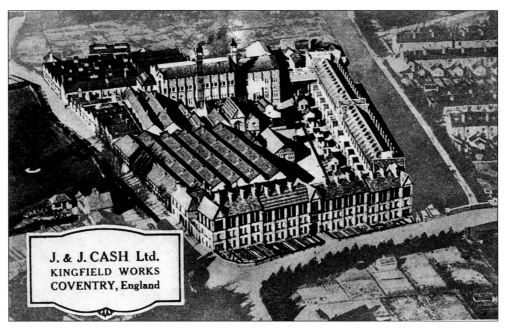

J&J Cash, Kingfield Road, Aerial View of Factory c1925 (Unknown)
Cash's Lane c1912 (WY)

The above advertising card clearly shows the sizeable factory that has grown up behind the original nineteenth century 'cottage factory' in Cash's Lane. The list of goods on the back illustrate some of the range of products then being made; *'shirt & coat labels, woven names and initials, black and coloured lutes, cigar and confectionery ribbon, washable trimmings for children's frocks hat ribbons and badges.'* The armed forces were also served well by Cash's for medal ribbons and uniform details. Below is the traditional view of Cash's factory from the Foleshill Road that hides the later developments behind the original 1857 factory. It is worth noting the Daimler car in the background that is likely to be out on test from the nearby car factory in Sandy Lane.

Leigh Mills, Hill Street c1910 (WY)
Leigh Mills Weaving Room c1896

The opening of Leigh Mills in 1863 was an act of local enlightened aristocratic investment on a grand scale. With the serious hardships caused by the collapse of the silk weaving industry Lord Leigh of nearby Stoneleigh Abbey together with other local philanthropists financed the construction of a woollen mill in Hill Street, to provide work for the un-employed. Here woollen goods were produced such as serge and worsted. Leigh Mills continued to produce woollen goods until its closure in the 1960s. Its place has now been taken by a multi-storey car park named after the factory. The first view shows the (mainly female) workforce emerging from the small exit onto Hill Street. The second picture is more typical of a Lancashire industrial scene. Unlike most of the views in this book which are taken from postcards it comes from a fascinating late Victorian book promoting various Coventry industries called *Coventry Up To Date*.

Courtaulds, Foleshill Road c1908 (WY)
S. Courtaulds Ltd c1910 (Waterman)

These two views are a reminder of the recent end of almost ninety years of occupation by Courtaulds of this Coventry site. The ten acres of land have recently been cleared except for a few of the early office buildings on the Foleshill Road. It is a bit of a mystery as to why Samuel Courtauld decided to introduce his new artificial silk process to Coventry rather than the traditional textile areas of Yorkshire and Lancashire. Would the skills of the old silk weaving industry be transferable? There was certainly an excess of female labour that the factory required. Given the rather slack health and safety controls, it is worrying to think what effect those early chemical processes had on the 3000 workers employed by 1913. The first view, taken within a few years of the factory opening, shows the first phase of building before huge profits led to the 1913 expansion. The second view shows the back of the works looking along the canal to the bridge where the Foleshill Road crosses the canal.

WATCH-MAKING

Although good quality clocks and watches had been made in Coventry since the latter part of the 17th century, at the height of the industry between 1860-1890 watches were mainly being assembled from parts made throughout the city and from component makers in Prescot, Lancs. In 1874 White's directory lists 130 watch manufacturers, but also lists these same companies as watch finishers. Only a small number of balance, escapement, movement and other specialist parts makers were listed. It was this hand finishing aspect of the industry that brought about its decline, when cheap mass-produced clocks and watches began to flood into the country from Switzerland and America. Although the overhead expenses were small in many of the houses with top shops in Chapelfields and Earlsdon where most of the parts were made, nevertheless by 1894 soup kitchens could be found even in these districts. Only Williamson and Rotherham and Sons really moved with the times, the latter installing in 1880 a complete plant of watch making machinery after careful study of the methods and tools in use in Switzerland and America. By the turn of the century many of the previous watch workers had been absorbed into the now booming cycle industry. The few companies which remained used their expertise to diversify into making accessories such as speedometers and gauges for the motor cycle and car industries.

Rotherham & Sons, Spon Street, c1915 (Unknown)

Workers seen leaving the works in Spon Street during the 1914-18 War. At that time the plant had been placed at the disposal of the War Office and was producing in addition to clocks and watches, clock work fuses for munitions. Although all the factory buildings have now been demolished the arch through which the workers are emerging still exists next to the Windmill pub, together with the offices seen to the right of the arch which was originally the Rotherham family home.

H. Williamson, Lower Holyhead Road c1910 (Appleby)
(H. Williamson c1910, Lower Holyhead Road (Unknown))

Like Rotherham, H Williamson Ltd at their Errington Works laid out their factory and installed the latest equipment to try and match the cheaper imported clocks and watches from America and Switzerland. The top postcard shows mainly young girls finishing the assembly of watch movements. The lower postcard again shows mainly girls making the small parts for watches on lathes and bench drills driven from under the benches by belting. This postcard on the reverse indicates the company at that time was known as the Astral Watch and Clock Factory. The premises, not as big as the pictures seem to indicate, was not grandly located being in Lower Holyhead Road behind what is today the Co-op Funeral Parlour. Although they won a large contract to supply watches to the Forces during the First World War, they unlike Rotherham did not diversify and eventually closed in 1931. The building was demolished in the 1980's.

Rotherham's "Golden Slipper" Watch.

Rotherham's English Half-Hunter Watch.

These two illustrations from a 1920's Rotherham's catalogue show the type of pocket watches they were manufacturing at that time. The design of the Golden Slipper watchcase was such that it made the watch completely dust proof. The watches were fully made on the premises whereas earlier watchmakers only assembled parts manufactured on the 'domestic' system of home workshops.

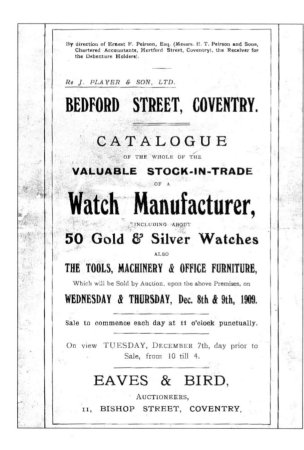

By direction of Ernest F. Peirson, Esq. (Messrs. E. T. Peirson and Sons, Chartered Accountants, Hertford Street, Coventry), the Receiver for the Debenture Holders).

Re J. PLAYER & SON, LTD.

BEDFORD STREET, COVENTRY.

CATALOGUE

OF THE WHOLE OF THE

VALUABLE STOCK-IN-TRADE

OF A

Watch Manufacturer,

INCLUDING ABOUT

50 Gold & Silver Watches

ALSO

THE TOOLS, MACHINERY & OFFICE FURNITURE,

Which will be Sold by Auction, upon the above Premises, on

WEDNESDAY & THURSDAY, Dec. 8th & 9th, 1909.

Sale to commence each day at 11 o'clock punctually.

On view TUESDAY, DECEMBER 7th, day prior to Sale, from 10 till 4.

EAVES & BIRD,

AUCTIONEERS,

11, BISHOP STREET, COVENTRY.

NEWSOME & Co,

14, BUTTS, COVENTRY

WHOLESALE EXPORT

Watch Manufacturers.

KEYLESS WATCHES

(CENTRE SECONDS),

¾-Plate and Full-Plate WATCHES,

ADJUSTED TO SUIT ALL CLIMATES.

Special Quotations given to Shippers.

WHOLESALE ONLY.

This advert from a late Victorian booklet shows the premises of Newsome and Company 14, The Butts. Another view can be seen on page 18.

By 1914 most of the watch companies had disappeared, only the Coventry Movement Company, Williamson and Rotherham who had moved into the special engineering field remained. In 1858 one of the leading watch manufacturers, J Player and Son started business. After the death of Joseph Player it was carried on by his son but eventually closed in 1909. The cover of the auction catalogue giving details of the sale at the Bedford Street premises (originally Butt's Lane) is indicated.

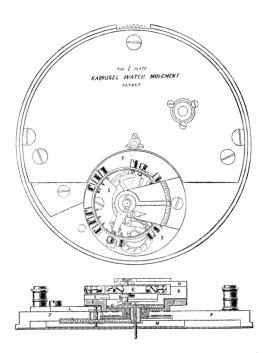

THE ¾ PLATE
KARRUSEL WATCH MOVEMENT
PATENT

This illustration shows a watch movement of the Tourbillon or Karrusel arrangement patented in 1893 by Bahne Bonniksen of 16, Norfolk Street. By allowing the balance to turn around itself the timing would remain constant whatever the attitude of the watch. His watches were of the finest made in the City and most other makers were soon fitting his balances into their watches.

ESTABLISHED 1750   R S   TRADE MARK

Rotherham & Sons Ltd.
Watch Manufacturers and Engineers
COVENTRY, England

Makers of all kinds of Specialities to the
**MOTOR, CYCLE, ELECTRICAL
AERO, GAS and ALLIED TRADES**
*LUBRICATORS, TAPS & VALVE WORK
FOR ALL KINDS OF MACHINERY*

Telegrams : : : : : Rotherhams, Coventry
Telephone Nos. : : : : : : 752 and 753
Codes : 5th Edition A.B.C. and Marconi International

LONDON OFFICE : 1, 2 & 3, HOLBORN CIRCUS. E.C.

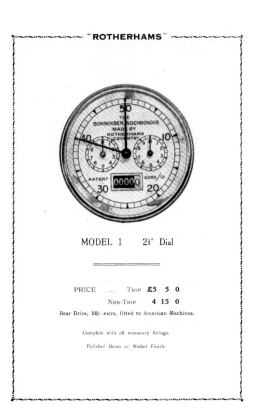

"ROTHERHAMS"

MODEL 1   2¾" Dial

PRICE   ...   TRIP £5 5 0
NON-TRIP   4 15 0
Rear Drive, 10/- extra, fitted to American Machines.

Complete with all necessary fittings.

Polished Brass or Nickel Finish.

"ROTHERHAMS"

A BONNIKSEN ISOCHRONOUS SPEEDOMETER
FITTED TO A MOTOR CYCLE

Like Rotherham, Bonniksen moved with the times at the ending of the watch industry, designing a speedometer for motor cycles. He made these himself for some time but by 1912 they were being manufactured for him and sold by Rotherham and Sons, as shown above.

BICYCLES, MOTORCYCLES AND MOTOR CARS

Although each of the above are grouped in separate sections, as a subject they are so interlinked that they must be considered together, as most of the major car makers of the 1930's had started by making bicycles and motorcycles.

Wheeled vehicles had been in existence for centuries but it was not until the early 19th century, in France, that the first two-wheeled machine was made which enabled a rider to propel himself along using his feet on the ground. This Hobby horse developed into the Boneshaker by the 1850's this machine having pedals on the front wheels. At this time in Coventry the sewing machine industry that had taken on many of the starving ribbon and silk workers, put out of employment by cheap French imports was itself in crisis due to the import of American sewing machines. In 1868 the Coventry Sewing Machine Company was asked by its agent in Paris to help with an order for Boneshakers for sale in France and was happy to oblige. Before long the works foreman James Starley incorporated many improvements. Eventually the Safety Cycle evolved basically to the design still in existence today. This meant that individuals could travel far greater distances under their own power than they could ever have achieved on foot. To enable even greater distances and more speed to be achieved with less physical effort, a petrol engine was soon added and later the vehicle was increased in size with four wheels to give full weather protection for two or more people. So from a very humble beginning a whole new industry came to Coventry.

BICYCLES

The Boneshaker 1869 (Unknown)

This picture is of the first Boneshaker made by the Coventry Sewing Machine Company in 1869. The Machine got its name as the 36 inch front and 30 inch rear wheels were of wooden construction fitted with iron tyres. Later the machines that weighed fifty-six pounds were fitted with wire-spoked wheels and solid rubber tyres that improved the ride.

Swift Motor Works, Little Park Street c1910 (Harvey Barton)

Where it all began. This was the Coventry Sewing Machine Company premises in Little Park Street, which became the Coventry Machinists Company in 1869. It was here that James Starley the works foremen's inventive genius was able to develop, until in 1870 together with William Hillman they set up their own business. At the time of this postcard the name of the company had again been changed becoming the Swift Cycle and Motor Company.

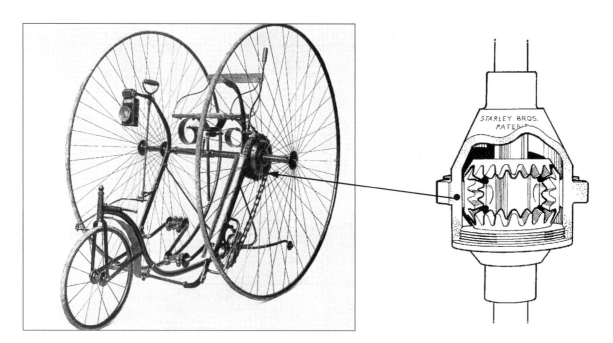

James Starley "Royal Salvo" 1879 (Unknown)

It was in 1877 that James Starley took out a patent for the *Royal Salvo* Tricycle as shown, which later developed into the *Meteor* Tricycle or *Sociable*. This name came into being as the width between the wheels enabled two people to sit side by side. To prevent the drive having to be offset to only one wheel, Starley also invented a differential gear, as seen on the right, this principle is the same as used in the motor industry to this day.

Starley Works, West Orchard c1885 (Unknown)

Before moving to the New Meteor Works in Queen Victoria Road, later to become the Rover Company, J K Starley, nephew of James Starley began making bicycles at the Old Meteor Works and Victoria Mills in West Orchard. In 1885 the new Rover Safety machine was introduced this being the forerunner of the modern bicycle. This picture shows early machines being produced at Victoria Mills. Two hoods over the brazing hearths can be seen, but very few tools other than files, handsaws, hammers and vices.

Humber Fire, Lower Ford Street 1896 (Unknown)

This picture taken from a glass negative shows all that remains of the Humber Cycle Company after the fire on 17th July 1896. Due to a close relationship with H J Lawson the workers were transferred to the 'Motor Mills' in Drapers Fields, later Daimler, whilst it was being rebuilt. It reopened in 1898 to make cars (See page 60)

The Butts Cycle Track c1890 (Unknown)

This cycle track was built in 1879 as a testing track for the many new types of bicycles being developed in the city. The picture illustrates a race between two Ariel machines patented by James Starley and William Hillman in 1870, which later developed into the Ordinary or Penny-Farthing. A later similar view of this cycle track is shown on page 49 of *TCWHL Vol. 2*.

Station Approach c1898 (Unknown)

This rare picture taken from a glass negative shows a cyclist riding towards Warwick Road from the Railway Station, which is just out of view on the right. Eaton Road is seen where the lady is walking. Coventry is still in the early days of making cars at this time the hoardings indicating such firms as Rudge-Whitworth, Calcott Brothers, Bayliss Thomas, Humber, Hobart Bird and Warman and Hazlewood all advertising cycles. The hoarding seen on the other side of Eaton Road indicating Allard and Company another cycle manufacturer in Earlsdon.

THE COVENTRY MACHINISTS' Co., Ld., COVENTRY.

DATE AS POSTMARK.

SUNDRIES AND REPAIRS DEPARTMENT.

Dear Sir,

We beg to acknowledge receipt of Swift Safety

and same shall have our best attention. In referring to

this please quote No. 383

Yours faithfully,

THE COVENTRY MACHINISTS' CO., LD.

This card sent to Oatlands Park, Surrey dated June 13th 1895 confirms the receipt of a Swift Safety Cycle. The machine had obviously been sent to the Coventry Machinists Company Ltd for repair.

Eiffel Tower Cycle 1895 (Unknown)

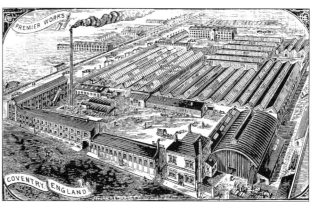

This illustration from a late Victorian book *'Coventry Up To Date'* shows the Premier Cycle Company Ltd. on the corner of Read Street and South Street. William Henry Herbert, brother of Alfred Herbert, and William Hillman, formed the original firm in 1875 to make sewing machines. After the failure of that industry they went into bicycle manufacture. To give some idea of the size of the bicycle industry at its height, this one firm alone made 21,000 bicycles in 1895 rising to 40,000 in 1897.

This is the first version of an Eiffel Tower Cycle built for Sam Brown by the Humber Cycle Company. Sam, who was born in Craven Street in 1875, had a larger machine built by Humber in 1894. This was 16ft high, weighed 133lbs and required a second rider positioned over the rear wheel to assist with the pedalling. After travelling all over the world giving demonstrations Sam retired from cycling in 1899 and went into the licence trade in Coventry.

Carrying out the advice of **Lord Roberts** to encourage rifle shooting, the **Harris** Cycle Co., Ltd , Coventry, are giving annually a **Silver Cup** and One Guinea to the 2nd Vol. Batt. Royal Warwickshire Regiment.

SERGT. W. TATLOW.
One of the Directors of the Harris Company, is well known throughout the United Kingdom as a crack shot. He has himself won a number of cups and trophies, and has taken part in the principal events at Bisley for many years.

PRIVATE C. GARDNER (WINNER, 1905-6)

Harris Cycle Company Ltd., Upper Well Street 1906 (Unknown)

This advertising postcard sent to a prospective customer in 1906 still has a Boer War influence about it. This must be one of several cards produced for advertising purposes as a similar card shows the late Dr Barnardo. The message on this card states that a donation is being sent to the Waifs and Strays Homes based upon the firm's output of cycles during 1906. The company operated from Hill Cross Works, 11, Upper Well Street.

Supplement to "CYCLING," June 26th, 1907.

G. A. OLLEY,
who has just broken the
1,000 MILES
UNPACED
RECORD
by 8 hrs. 57 mins. Monday, 17th June, 4 p.m., to Saturday, 22nd June, 1 a.m., 4 days 9 hours.

Mr. Olley rode a Rudge - Whitworth No. 542 "Speed-Iron," with Fagan
2-Speed Gear and Celluloid-covered Handle-bars. Weight, 22 lbs. all on.

For Important Notice, P.T.O.

TEMPLE PRESS LTD., LONDON, E C.

Rudge-Whitworth Ltd, Crow Lane 1907 (Temple Press Ltd)

This postcard issued as a supplement to the *Cycling* magazine on 26th June 1907, gives details of their *Speed Iron* machine, on which Mr G A Olley had just broken the thousand miles record. Modern cyclists will scoff at the time of four days nine hours taken but bearing in mind the type and weight of machine together with the state of the roads at the time, it must have been quite an achievement. Rudge at their Crow Lane Works went on to become a giant in motorcycle manufacture and racing (See page 53).

O'Brien Building, Foleshill Road near Cash's Lane c1910 (Unknown)

This advertising postcard shows the building built in 1906 by Edgar O'Brien to build Coventry Challenge Bicycles. The building still exists mainly unaltered but for the addition of air raid shelters on the front, but is not as big as the tram travelling down Foleshill Road would signify. Later under Edward O'Brien it became, as is stated, The World's Largest Cycle Dealer. The advert on the left indicates the many other makes of bicycle available in addition to the Challenge.

Singer and Company Ltd, Canterbury Street c1912 (Unknown)

This advertising postcard is of another company who began making bicycles then went on to make motorcycles and cars. Founded in 1874 by George Singer, the company traded from large premises in Canterbury Street, which still exists although now converted to a Coventry University halls of residence site. Car production began in 1902 with the manufacture of a Tri-Car and by the time of this postcard were also making the successful Singer Ten, both of which are shown on the card.

Humber Works, Stoke 1922 (Unknown)

Both of these pictures were taken in the North Wing Block at the Humber Stoke works. Although over-production of bicycles in the late 1890's made many companies turn to motorcycle and car production, Humber still carried on producing bicycles until the late 1930's. To give some idea of the large number still being made in 1922 the top view shows the cycle wheel building shop, whilst the lower view is of the handlebar and accessory stores.

MOTORCYCLES

Swift Motor Tricycle 1899 (Unknown)

Although the motor vehicle industry started in Germany the first motorised bicycle was produced in this country. At the 1884 Stanley Cycle Show at Blackfriars Bridge in London, Edward Butler exhibited drawings of a motor tricycle which he built and ran later that year. A tricycle based upon established bicycle practise was favoured as the drive from the engine could be taken to the rear wheels via a differential. Direct drive to a single rear wheel was considered unsafe as sideslip made riding on wet roads very hair-raising. The Swift machine shown was considered one of the best made here or in France.

Pennington Motor Tandem, The Butts 1897 (Unknown)

E J Pennington arrived in this country from America in 1896 making extravagant claims for a motorised bicycle powered by a paraffin engine. Although he was paid a large sum of money for his patents by H J Lawson of the Great Horseless Carriage Company only two machines, one a tandem, were made, by Humber Ltd at their Lower Ford Street Works. Although large orders were placed based upon false advertising, as the performance did not live up to that claimed, no more were made. The picture shows the tandem being demonstrated at The Butts cycle track.

Humber Electric Tandem, Lower Ford Street 1898 (Unknown)

This interesting machine first exhibited at the Stanley bicycle show in November 1897 was operated by an electric motor powered from accumulators. Although it operated well on the racetrack, on the road the accumulators proved to be too heavy and could not carry sufficient energy to operate for long periods.

Singer Motor Cycle Wheel, Canterbury Street 1901 (Unknown)

This interesting design of motorised bicycle was developed by Perks and Birch of Coventry, later taken up by the Singer Bicycle Company in 1901. Incorporating a 2 HP engine the whole mechanism including the petrol tank was arranged inside the aluminium spoked backwheel. Being manufactured successfully for a number of years it incorporated magneto ignition probably the first 'motor' bicycle to do so.

Triumph Motor Bicycle, Priory Street 1902 (Unknown)

The invention of the V Belt in 1902 brought about the death of the motor tricycle in favour of the motor cycle. The picture is of a Triumph machine fitted with a 2 HP Minerva engine placed low in the frame. The lower centre of gravity and flexible drive to the real wheel brought about by the belt overcame the sideslip problem and set the design standard which has remained to this day.

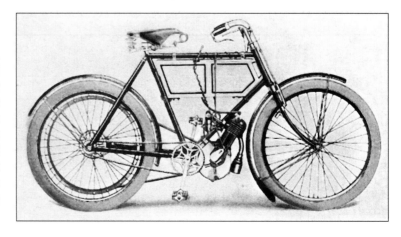

Humber Works, Stoke 1911 (Unknown)
Humber Twin, 1911 (Jackson and Son)

The upper picture is in the Humber works at Stoke and shows motor cycles in course of manufacture. By the look of the frame and front forks it would seem that the model being produced is the 350cc Twin. The man on the extreme left of the picture is Sam Wright who is shown in the lower view testing a 350cc Twin at the Butts Cycle track. Later in June 1911 he went to Brooklands where he took part in the Junior One-Hour T.T Race on the same machine. It is interesting that he also raced cars for Humber (See page 61)

Triumph Team, Isle of Man 1914 (Unknown)

Triumph was very active in motorcycle racing prior to the First World War. This postcard shows their team at the 1914 Tourist Trophy Race at Ramsey, Isle of Man. Humber must also have entered as Sam Wright can be seen over the second rider from the right with other members of the team.

This triumph advert is from the 1911 Godiva Procession programme.

Singer, Canterbury Street c1912 (Unknown)

Although posed in a studio this postcard shows a very clear picture of a single cylinder machine with belt drive as produced by Singer in about 1912. The generator for the Carbide lamps can be seen at the rear of the handlebars.

Rudge-Whitworth, Crow Lane 1911 (Unknown)

The two advertising postcards shown here are typical of details being sent out by Rudge to prospective customers at that time.

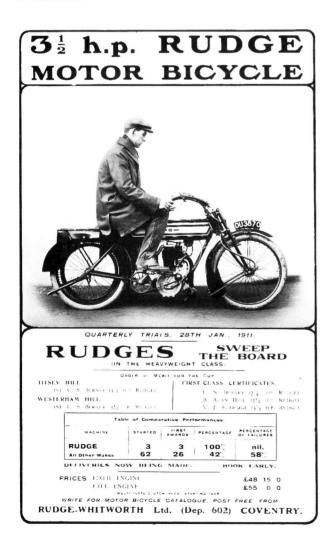

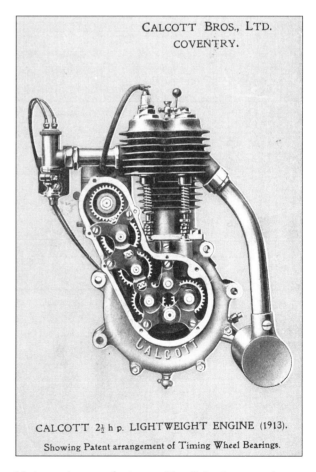

CALCOTT 2½ h p. LIGHTWEIGHT ENGINE (1913).

Showing Patent arrangement of Timing Wheel Bearings.

Motorcycle manufacturers, like Calcott, were always trying to advertise any design improvements as a way to gain orders from their competitors.

"EXCELSIOR" 5-6 h.p. Big Single, climbing Stoneleigh Hill, with Side Car and EIGHT up. Total load of passengers, 12 cwt. 1 qr. Combined weight, 18 cwt. 14 lbs. Gears—4, 7¾ and 13 to 1

Three advertising postcards, the first pre First World War. The one to the left is showing a procession float with a 1925 Coventry Victor Flat Twin machine. The bottom picture illustrates a lightweight Coventry Eagle *Marvel* machine the postcard being postmarked 1931.

MOTORCARS

Taylor, Cooper and Bednall Car 1894 (Unknown)

Although Daimler is credited with making the first car in Coventry during 1896, as early as 1888 Starley produced a small electrically propelled Tri-Car at his Meteor Works in West Orchard. In 1894 Taylor, Cooper and Bednall made the first four-wheel car as shown, being powered by electric accumulators. This car, however, did not go into production as not until the Red Flag Act, that restricted vehicles to 4 MPH, was repealed in August 1896, were cars of this type viable.

The First Daimler 1896 (Unknown)

H J Lawson, undoubtedly the father of the British motor industry, had already floated the Great Horseless Carriage Company when the Red Flag Act was repealed. Soon afterwards the first Daimler, a two cylinder, 6 HP Wagonette with tiller steering, seen above, was produced at the Coventry Cotton Mills in Drapers Fields from parts imported from Germany. By the following year they were turning out cars fully manufactured at the Motor Mills, the name by which it was then known.

Daimler Works, Sandy Lane c1908 (Harvey Barton)
General View of Daimler Works c1907 (Maule and Co.)

This postcard shows the original Cotton Mill building after conversion to a three-tier machine shop for producing parts for early Daimler cars. This is the side view of the same building shown on page 68 of *TCWHL Vol 2*. The workers are walking towards the main gateway on Sandy Lane. In the lower view showing the whole 12.5-acre site the same side view of the Cotton Mill building can be seen on the right. The roofs of the car assembly buildings are seen in the middle with the higher roof of the office building at the Sandy Lane gateway on the extreme left. The gardens in the foreground are at the rear of Merrick Lodge in St Nicholas Street. In 1937 this site was vacated, the Radford Works becoming the main works. In 1940 in the Blitz most of the buildings including the old Cotton Mill were destroyed.

COPYRIGHT.   **GENERAL VIEW OF DAIMLER WORKS, COVENTRY.**   PHOTO BY
MAULE & CO., COVENTRY.
COMPRISING SHOPPING COVERING 12½ ACRES OF GROUND.

A TYPICAL WEEK'S OUTPUT OF DAIMLER MOTOR CARS.

COPYRIGHT PHOTO BY MAULE & CO , COVENTRY.

Daimler Motor Cars, Sandy Lane c1906 (Maule and Co.)
Daimler Car c1908 (Unknown)

By 1906 Daimler had evolved from the original Great Horseless Carriage Company, producing a copy of a German car in 1896, into The Daimler Motor Company (1904) Ltd producing a true British designed car. In the interim due to generous legislation French cars imported into the country were far superior in design to contemporary English models. By 1907 lessons had been learned and the Daimler models then being produced in every way surpassed French vehicles. The advertising postcard above shows a typical weeks output at Daimler in 1906. By 1907 this had increased to 'forty cars of the highest class per week', mentioned in the official Godiva Procession programme of that year. Although small in number by today's standards these cars were of the best available in the country, being supplied to rich customers, including Royalty. The postcard below gives an indication of the type of car and superior specification being offered at the time. The central headlight seems odd but must have been normal practice at Daimler, as several cars in the above picture have the same arrangement.

Daimler, Radford Works 1913 (Unknown)
Inside Radford Works 1913 (Unknown)

The first postcard is a view looking down the main drive from the Daimler Road gateway. The small gatehouse and weighbridge seen on the right were later demolished with a new gatehouse, fire station and office block being built on the left where the timber planks are laying. Two Daimler buses with solid tyre wheels are seen waiting to take workers into the centre of the city. The lower view is taken inside the main car assembly shop with vehicles in various stages of production. Very soon after this picture was taken this area would be turned over to the manufacture of munitions. (See page 77)

Rover Car at New Meteor Works, Rover Road 1907 (Unknown)
Rover T.T. Winner 1907 (Unknown)

The name Rover was originally used for the Safety Bicycle designed by J K Starley nephew of James Starley. When the firm moved into the New Meteor works from their old works in West Orchard and started to manufacture cars the name Rover was adopted for the new vehicles. The Garfield Road entrance to the works from Queen Victoria Road can be seen on page 11 of *TCWHL Vol 2*. The top postcard shows a 20 HP car being prepared at the works, for the 1907 International Tourist Trophy Race. The man seated in the car is the eventual winner and can also be seen in the lower picture. This shows the winning car number 22, Reg. No. DU 1086 after the race on May 30th together with the trophy they received. Another Rover car, number 25, was also entered and finished not far behind the winner

The Trophy.

20 h.p. ROVER—THE WINNING CAR.

THE INTERNATIONAL TOURIST TROPHY RACE, May 30, 1907.

Humber Works, Lower Ford Street c1906 (Harvey Barton)

This view is of the main entrance to the Humber Works on the corner of Lower Ford Street and All Saints Lane. The premises had been the Humber Cycle Company Works until a major fire occurred on the 17th July 1896. After it had been rebuilt Humber began making cars here in 1898. When the company moved to the Stoke works in 1908 these premises were taken over by B.T.H. (See page 85)

Hall in Main Office Block, Humber Works, Stoke c1920 (Unknown)

The entrance hall at Humber, Stoke Works showing some of the items made at Humber during the 1914-18 War. In the archway to the left is a nine cylinder W O Bentley BR2 rotary engine with the company roll of honour in the next archway. A third scale model of an Avro 504 hangs from the ceiling and gun carriages also made in large numbers are seen either side of the stairs.

Humber Works, Stoke c1914 (Unknown)
Humber T.T. Team, Isle of Man 1914 (Unknown)

The postcard above shows the Guarantee Dept. at Humber Stoke works just before the First World War. Many different models are being worked on, the one in the foreground having been completely stripped down to the chassis. Humber were very involved in promoting their production models by entering races, including the Royal Automobile Club International Tourist Trophy Race in the Isle of Man. The three cars they entered for the 1914 race are shown in the lower postcard outside the Mitre Hotel at Douglas. Sam Wright who drove car number 20 in the race is seen standing behind the car. Of the three cars entered, number 20 did best, retiring on the fourteenth of the sixteen-lap race. The card sent to his wife from Kirkmichael said that in practice he had been lapping in 43 minutes. The race was won by a Sunbeam in 10 hours 36 minutes with a Minerva coming second, eight minutes behind.

Hotchkiss Factory, Gosford Street 1922 (Unknown)

This view taken six years after the factory was built is taken from an almost identical position to that showing its construction, see page 19 *TCWHL Vol 1*. The picture shows one day's delivery of fifty, 11.9 HP engine and gearbox units starting out for the Morris works at Cowley, Oxfordshire. At this time twenty thousand engines of various types had been manufactured in the three years since the end of the 1914-18 War. In 1923 the works were acquired by William Morris, later becoming Morris Motors Ltd, Engines Branch.

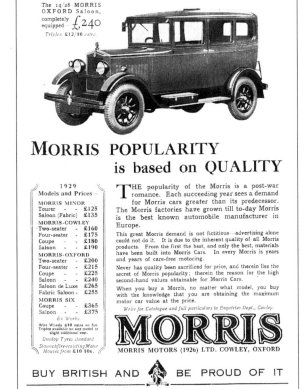

This advert from the official programme of the 1929 Lady Godiva Procession and Pageant shows the Morris range of cars available that year. Although not built in Coventry the engines and gearboxes were still being made at the Engines Branch shown above. The bodies were also being made at the Bodies Branch at Quinton Road also established in 1926 by William Morris.

CANLEY WORKS

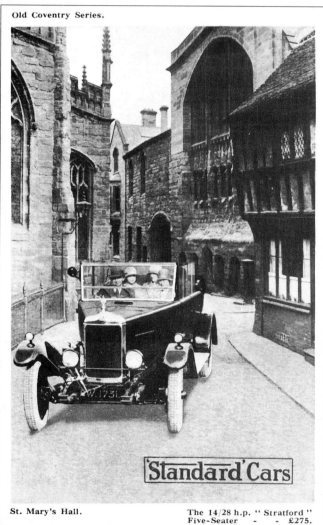

Old Coventry Series.

St. Mary's Hall.

The 14/28 h.p. " Stratford "
Five-Seater - - £275.

'Standard' Cars

Standard Motor Company Ltd, Canley Works 1932 (Unknown)

The Standard Motor Company was one firm who from the word go made motor cars, the first vehicle being produced in 1903 at their Much Park Street Works. The firm expanded very rapidly acquiring several premises including the old Duryea Motor Company works in Widdrington Road, later to become Coventry Climax. The Canley works were built early in the First World War to produce aeroplanes in large numbers, 1600 being made by the end of the war. When car production was started at Canley, the other premises were vacated, the original works in Much Park Street becoming Charlesworth Bodies Ltd. The postcard above shows the office block at Canley known as Ivy Cottage, which has only recently been demolished. The advertising postcard shown to the left is of the 14/28 HP *Stratford* five-seater first introduced in 1928. Like most car firms in the early 1930s Standard had trading problems but under the leadership of Captain J P Black expanded and was in a strong position at the start of the Second World War to again produce planes and other war materials in large quantity.

63

AIRCRAFT

Although some aircraft had been built in Coventry before the First World War, it was the fact that so many major engineering and car firms were well established at the start of hostilities that government contracts were placed for building both aircraft and engines. Daimler, Humber, Siddeley Deasey and Standard were the main recipients of these contracts. The Daimler Company in particular were quick to respond to the war needs, signing an agreement with the French Gnome engine company in the first week of the war to produce their 80 HP seven cylinder rotary engine. They promised to have an engine running within eight weeks of receiving a sample engine. When it was received it was stripped down, drawings made, materials acquired, the parts manufactured and assembled. A special test rig was also manufactured and the engine was started up with one hour to spare. Later a 250 HP nine-cylinder BR2 rotary engine designed by W O Bentley was produced, three hundred and thirty nine of these engines being delivered in one month alone at the latter stage of the war. In addition an airfield needed to be built at the rear of the Radford works to enable the large number of aircraft produced to be test flown. The Standard Company also had to build a special works at Canley in 1916 to enable aircraft to be manufactured. By the armistice no fewer than 1,600 RE8 and BE12 together with Sopwith Pup and Camel machines had been produced. With the ending of the war, production of aircraft and engines ceased with the exception of one company, Siddeley Deasey who had produced the 6-cylinder BHP water-cooled engine during the war had redesigned it to become the Puma. This, together with the Siskin aircraft brought out later with the Armstrong Siddeley Jaguar engine, laid the foundations of this very successful company, who after acquiring the old RAF flying field at Whitley in 1920 went on to design many wonderful aircraft. These included the bomber named after the airfield that did such noble service during the Second World War. (See page 72) Although now merged with Rolls Royce the expertise built up since the First World War still lives on at Ansty.

Humber Works, Stoke 1910 (Unknown)

In 1909 the Humber Company announced that it was to start building aircraft of the Bleriot XI type. Although this postcard dated 1910 shows several Bleriot machines being assembled at the Humber works, aircraft production had ceased by 1912. In addition to the Bleriot, which was fitted with a 25 HP 3-cylinder semi-radial Humber engine, Humber, Le Blon and Lovelace monoplanes together with Sommer biplanes were also produced.

This 1910 advert gives an indication of the price of aeroplanes being manufactured by Humber. The auction notice opposite, placed in the August 24th 1912 edition of *Flight* magazine, shows that Humber were giving up the manufacture of aeroplanes so soon after being involved in their production.

Humber Ltd 1912 (Unknown)

This postcard dated 22nd June 1912 shows a Humber Biplane with a 50 HP 4-cylinder Humber water-cooled engine. The pilot is indicated as being S V Setti but whether he is the owner or is demonstrating the machine to a prospective buyer is not known. Only two months later all of the Humber stock of aircraft, engines and parts were to be auctioned.

This advert in a 1912 edition of *Flight* magazine shows that Coventry Ordnance could design both monoplanes and biplanes to meet the needs of Naval and Military services, though the information below suggests otherwise.

Coventry Ordnance, Salisbury Plain 1912 (Unknown)

During August 1912 a Military Aeroplane Competition was held at Larkhill Aerodrome, Salisbury Plain to evaluate current machines for possible military use. Of the 32 machines that took part Coventry Ordnance entered two, the one illustrated flown by Raynham being powered by a 110 HP Chenu Water Cooled engine. At the trials they did not perform well and Coventry Ordnance did not proceed with aeroplane manufacture.

French Gnome Engine, Daimler Radford Works 1914 (Unknown)

This picture shows the first 80 HP seven cylinder Gnome rotary engine produced by Daimler in the first two months of the Great War, ready for its first test run. When the propeller had been fitted and it was first started in the dark the crowd who witnessed the event stated that with the flames issuing from the open exhaust ports of the rotating cylinders, it was reminiscent of a huge Catherine Wheel.

W O Bentley BR1 Engine, Humber Works, Stoke 1915 (Humber Ltd)

Although Daimler were producing the 80 HP Gnome seven cylinder rotary engine, W O Bentley designed a nine cylinder rotary engine, the early BR1 being produced by Humber Ltd. The first engine is seen on its rig ready for testing. Humber and Daimler built the BR1 and the later BR2 engine that produced 250 HP. Daimler alone between June and December 1918 produced 1,245 of these engines.

BR2 Engine on Balancing Test Rig, Humber Works, Stoke 1918 (Unknown)

As the concept of the rotary engine is that the crankshaft is stationary and the whole engine together with the propeller rotate, the engine must be finely balanced. It is seen here on its special rig about to be rotated on rollers. If out of balance the aircraft would have vibration and control problems.

Daimler Aeroplane Assembly Shop, Radford 1916 (Unknown)
Daimler Radford Aerodrome 1916 (Unknown)

As well as making Gnome engines Daimler also produced the 70 HP RAF 1A engine this being an eight cylinder air-cooled V unit on the lines of the French Renault. At the same time the company were also producing the BE2C plane in their recently constructed aeroplane shop. It was soon realised that to test the machines a flight ground was necessary, so an area behind the Radford Works was cleared of trees and hedges and the ground levelled out. The first view shows BE2C airframes in course of manufacture. The second view shows the first BE2C machine with RAF IA engine being prepared for its initial flight. The aerodrome survived for some years after the war. On Saturday 9th June 1923 the Hospital Carnival Procession started from this venue. (See page 67 *TCWHL Vol 2*) Older residents in the Capmartin Road area still refer to the Radford Aerodrome Estate as all the houses were built on the airfield site.

Aero-engine Strippers, Siddeley Deasey Works, Cheylesmore 1918 (Taylor Bros)

Late in 1915, Siddeley Deasey began to engage female labour and by the end of 1917 this included a large number of Belgian workers. As well as manufacturing aero-engines a large number were sent back to the works for repair. The girls in the picture thought to be Belgian were used as 'grease monkeys' to strip these engines ready for inspection and repair. It is known that the works manager Mr A G Asbury paid for photographs to be taken when the Belgian girls left at the end of the war and as this picture is dated 1918 it is thought that this is one of these photographs.

Siddeley Puma Engine c1920 (Unknown)

This is the six-cylinder water-cooled BHP (Beardmore, Halford, Pollinger) aero-engine after it had been completely redesigned by Mr F R Smith of Siddeley Deasey to become the Puma. This engine fitted to the DH4 Biplane became the mainstay of the British bombing force in the latter stages of the Great War. By the end of the war it had been produced in greater numbers than any other aero-engine in England, 160 per week in the last few months. This production held up the new 14 cylinder radial engine which became the Jaguar Major, later fitted successfully to the Siskin.

The Prototype Siskin Aircraft, Whitley 1920 (Siddeley Deasey)

First begun in 1919 this machine built of wood and canvas was the first aircraft to be designed and constructed by the Siddeley Deasey Company from experience gained building RE7, RE8, SE5 and DH9 aircraft in the 1914-18 War. Later developed to an all-steel construction and fitted with a 385HP Armstrong Siddeley Jaguar Major Engine the Siskin III was a revolutionary aircraft for its day. It became the RAF's standard single seat fighter being the first all steel aircraft in the world to go into series production. In all 214 aircraft were delivered to British and Commonwealth countries.

Siskin III at Whitley 1924 (Unknown)

This is the Siskin III fitted with a 385 HP Jaguar Major engine that did the fastest time and came second in the 1924 Kings Cup air race, seen after returning to Whitley. The machine G-EBJQ was flown by Captain Jones, born at 10 Little Butcher Row, who after joining the Royal Warwickshire Regiment transferred to the RFC in 1916 qualifying as a pilot. A Siskin III had won the Kings Cup in 1923 and again went on to win the race in 1925. The picture shows flight shed foreman Goldsmith and his assistant Ambler standing in the foreground on either side of the machine.

Whitley Abbey Aerodrome c1930 (Unknown)

These two illustrations give an indication of the size of Whitley Abbey aerodrome in the 1930's. At the time of the upper photograph Hawker Hart Aircraft would be in the course of manufacture in the hangers in the foreground. The Siskin III seen in the lower picture on page 70 is standing in front of hanger 3 which is at the far end on the left in the upper picture. To the left of this hanger the buildings with the four gabled roofs are the flight sheds. The aerodrome was built in the First World War by German prisoners for the RFC, later the RAF. It was purchased in 1920 by Sir W G Armstrong Whitworth Aircraft Ltd. and is now the Jaguar Cars engineering centre. The maps below show the layout and the facilities that were available at the aerodrome.

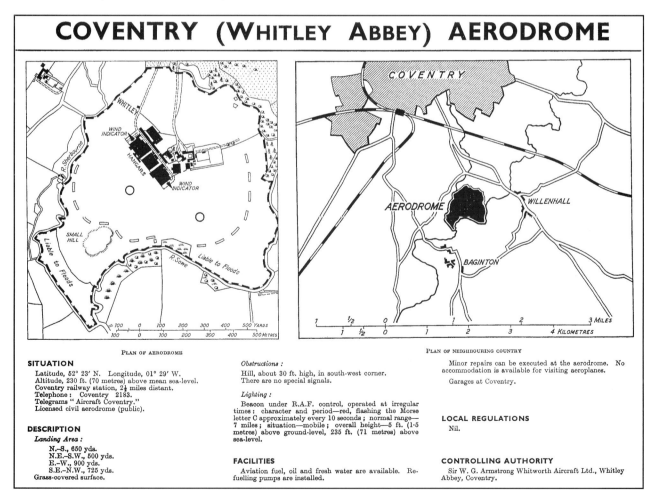

COVENTRY (WHITLEY ABBEY) AERODROME

PLAN OF AERODROME

PLAN OF NEIGHBOURING COUNTRY

SITUATION

Latitude, 52° 23' N. Longitude, 01° 29' W.
Altitude, 230 ft. (70 metres) above mean sea-level.
Coventry railway station, 2¼ miles distant.
Telephone : Coventry 2183.
Telegrams " Aircraft Coventry."
Licensed civil aerodrome (public).

DESCRIPTION

Landing Area :

N.–S., 650 yds.
N.E.–S.W., 500 yds.
E.–W., 900 yds.
S.E.–N.W., 725 yds.
Grass-covered surface.

Obstructions :

Hill, about 30 ft. high, in south-west corner.
There are no special signals.

Lighting :

Beacon under R.A.F. control, operated at irregular times : character and period—red, flashing the Morse letter C approximately every 10 seconds ; normal range—7 miles ; situation—mobile ; overall height—5 ft. (1·5 metres) above ground-level, 235 ft. (71 metres) above sea-level.

FACILITIES

Aviation fuel, oil and fresh water are available. Re-fuelling pumps are installed.

Minor repairs can be executed at the aerodrome. No accommodation is available for visiting aeroplanes.

Garages at Coventry.

LOCAL REGULATIONS

Nil.

CONTROLLING AUTHORITY

Sir W. G. Armstrong Whitworth Aircraft Ltd., Whitley Abbey, Coventry.

Wolf Crash at Whitley 1931 (Unknown)

Soon after the 1914-18 War contracts were placed with four principal aircraft manufacturers to establish flying schools. This was to enable RAF reserve officers to put in their compulsory annual flying hours. Sir W G Armstrong Whitworth Aircraft Ltd was one of those chosen and the school was opened at Whitley Abbey Aerodrome in 1923. Three, two seat Wolf trainer biplanes were designed and built by the company with 350 HP Jaguar II Engines, being used until the school was transferred to Hamble in 1932. The one seen above G-EBHJ being flown by F O Burton made a forced landing at Whitley on 15th January 1931 and was not rebuilt.

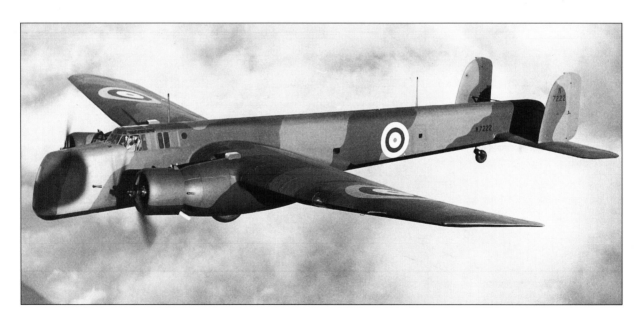

Armstrong Whitworth Whitley c1938 (Unknown)

The first Whitley was powered by Armstrong Siddeley Tiger engines and first flew on the 17th March 1936. It was the first all-metal stressed skin aircraft to go into production. It was also the first Royal Air Force aircraft to have a retractable undercarriage. The machine shown is a Mark II with Tiger engines, later Mark IV and V machines had Rolls Royce Merlin engines. The Whitley that went on to give noble service during the war did have one early distinction in that it was the first aircraft to bomb Berlin on the night of 1st-2nd October 1939.

MUNITIONS/ARMAMENTS

Before this century Coventry has never had much of tradition for producing munitions or armaments apart from at times of war. Yet its record in two world wars shows a startling capacity to meet the huge demands made on its industrial expertise. Only the Coventry Ordnance Works, set up by a shipbuilding consortium, was solely involved in making weapons before the First World War. Nevertheless the city's experience in engineering made it a natural base for various types of munitions work and it became a government designated munitions centre. Most of the large car firms had already experimented with aircraft production before 1914 and soon attracted government contracts to provide for the new military tactic of aerial warfare. Not surprisingly, various military vehicles were also produced but some firms such as Rover were considered to have a car that was too light for military use and therefore forced to turn most of its wartime production to mortars, shells and fuses. Rudge Whitworth faced a similar situation but also produced .303 rifle ammunition. However, all firms producing munitions were overshadowed by the operations of White and Poppe in Holbrooks. It was a relatively small engineering firm at the start of the war but by 1918 it was employing 11,000 people at three different sites. After the war many of the firms went back to their pre-war specialisms, but some such as Siddeley Deasy continued and linked up with Armstrong Whitworth to be a major force in aircraft development and production. They also continued to produce cars until the 1950s.

Ordnance Works New Extension, c1907 (Cooke)

Although engineering work had been carried out on this site since the 1890s it was only with the end of various mergers and take-overs in 1906 that Coventry Ordnance Works Ltd was born. This was to be a significant armaments factory serving the needs, amongst others, of several Scottish naval dockyards. Given the naval arms race with Germany that was taking place at that time it is rather ironic that the contract for the huge new extension to the factory was given to a German firm. The workshop was supposedly the largest in Europe. The view is near the junction of Newdegate Street and Red Lane by the canal. House building is apparent in readiness for the influx of new employees.

Ordnance Works Field Guns c1914 (T-H Co)
Ordnance Works Wood Mill c1907 (Cooke)

This first view shows one bay of the large extension given over to the construction of field guns and ammunition trailers. This was not the main function of this area, which was for the production of massive naval guns. The factory had been producing a number of field guns from its earliest days, but most famously 4.5-inch howitzers for the army. Between 1909 and 1914 it had only made 182 but in the next few years production totalled 3,000. The guns were still in use at the end of the Second World War. The second view shows the extensive wood mill operation that was necessary for the production of the gun carriage and the ammunition carrier shown in the first picture; all horse drawn of course. Most of this work was done in the original factory in Ordnance Road. The production of wooden wheels was another element of this work with a record of 250 being produced in one day during the First World War.

Turning the Barrels, Ordnance Works c1914 (T-H Co)
Turning the Barrels, Ordnance Works c1914 (T-H Co)

The scale of the work tackled at the Ordnance Works is well illustrated by these views of the giant lathes used to turn the barrels of the naval guns into shape. They were very complex and difficult weapons to produce and some would be so valuable they would be reused in future warships when their original homes were scrapped. The steel used in the manufacture of the barrels would be brought from Sheffield. They would then be shaped by the machines shown here in the new workshop extension, while elsewhere equally large wire winding machines were used to make the cores for the barrels. The first large naval guns of more than 50 tons and 13.5 inch bore, illustrated here, were produced in 1911. By 1914 even larger guns, nicknamed 'Big Lizzie' were being produced at the works, these were 100 tons and 15 inch bore. In 1915 on the instructions of Winston Churchill, one of these largest guns was deployed for land use in France as an attempt to break the trench warfare stalemate.

75

Naval Gun Housing, Ordnance Works c1914 (T-H Co)
Transporting the Gun Barrels, Ordnance Works c1914 (T-H Co)

The size of the naval guns that were constructed can be judged by the view shown here and by comparing them to the man standing besides the shells designed for the guns. This would be a temporary construction to check that the barrels would fit properly into their housing. A good rail connection was essential for moving the barrels, as it would be almost impossible to transport by road. Fortunately the neighbouring Webster Brickworks had developed a branch line to the Coventry-Nuneaton Railway which the Ordnance Works used until 1916, famously blocking the Stony Stanton Road every time a consignment passed. Part of the way through the war a more convenient connection was made with the eastern loop line. This view shows a 13.5-inch gun ready for delivery. After being sent for test firing (originally to Lincolnshire) they would then be taken to Glasgow for fitting in the Clyde shipyards.

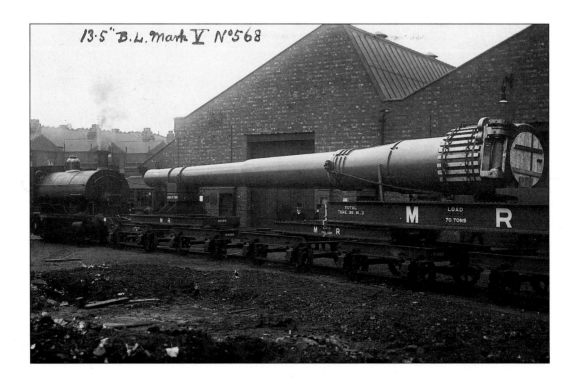

Daimler Company, Radford Works c1916
Munitions Workers (Canary Girls), Coventry Munitions Ltd, Far Gosford Street c1916 (Unknown)

The top view is of the same building shown on page 58 used for building cars in peacetime. Here it is being used for the production of 12 inch shells; 2000 a week at the height of war. The shells did not travel far for the next stage in the production process for many factories large and small had government contracts for putting the explosive into the shells. The second picture shows some of the women who did this work who had been attracted to Coventry by the relatively high wages, coming from as far afield as Ireland. They would work very long shifts doing various manual tasks associated with the munitions industry. For many this meant filling shells with TNT. Health and safety rules were very slack and the lack of protective clothing meant that the women suffered from toxic jaundice. The resulting yellow colour of their skin earned them the nickname of 'canary girls'. Coventry Munitions Ltd were one of a number of new companies set up that barely lasted the duration of the war.

Hotchkiss & Cie, Gosford Street c1915 (Unknown)
Hotchkiss & Cie, Gosford Street c1920 (Unknown)

Next door to the Coventry Munitions Factory, shown on the previous page, were the first premises of Hotchkiss & Cie, a French firm, famous for their machine guns. This first view shows their temporary headquarters while the new factory (built by the government and leased to Hotchkiss), shown in the second picture was being built alongside. The soldiers guarding the entrance were a common sight outside many factories in Coventry involved with munitions work. By the end of the war the Hotchkiss factory had produced 50,000 of their heavy machine guns, but began to wind down their armament work in favour of engines. The factory had continued to expand during this period and had even expanded into premises on the other side of Gosford Street. The medieval facade of shops concealed a rabbit warren of industrial premises along the length of this ancient street. One of the companies Hotchkiss made engines for, Morris Motors, took over the company in the 1920s. The converted factory is now Coventry University's Business School.

Hotchkiss Works
Coventry

MACHINE TOOLS

Ever since the start of the bicycle industry in the 1860s there grew up a secondary industry of component suppliers supporting the major manufacturers. It was always more convenient to buy in certain parts rather than make the whole machine. But all the factories required specialist machines on which to make these parts. As the engineering technology became more complex the construction of machine tools became more specialised. Ironically the depressions of the inter-war years were a boost for Coventry's machine tool manufacturers. Engineering firms were looking for ways to cut costs during this difficult period and investment in machinery meant that labour could be cut. Firms such as Alfred Herbert, Coventry Gauge & Tool, Webster & Bennett and Wickman flourished during this period. A huge stimulus came towards the end of the 1930s from the government plans for rearmament against the threat from Germany. With the technological developments that war demanded, an adequate supply of machine tools was to be essential.

Herbert and Hubbard, Upper York Street c1889 (Unknown)

This view shows the inside of the original Herbert and Hubbard workshop.

Alfred Herbert Ltd, Upper York Street c1914 (Unknown)

It was in 1889 that Alfred Herbert with an old school friend William Hubbard started a small business in Upper York Street under the name of Herbert and Hubbard to manufacture machines connected to the cycle trade. Within a short time it became Alfred Herbert Ltd eventually growing into the largest machine tool making firm in Europe. The postcard below shows workers leaving the enlarged works in Upper York Street walking towards The Butts. In 1930 when the firm moved to their larger Edgwick Works, the Butts premises were taken over by Modern Machine Tools.

ALFRED HERBERT LTD. COVENTRY

MAKERS OF MACHINE TOOLS, SMALL TOOLS, AND MACHINE SHOP ACCESSORIES.

AN IMPORTANT COVENTRY INDUSTRY.

A FEW facts about our new works at Coventry :—

Total area of site - 37 acres.

Total area of buildings 17 acres.

3000 Coventry workpeople are employed.

1300 machine tools in the plant.

1500 machine tools available for immediate delivery.

WE INVITE ALL ENGINEERS HAVING A PROPER INTEREST IN MACHINE TOOLS, TO VISIT OUR WORKS.

Herbert No. 20 Combination Turret Lathe set up for machining large lathe spindles, exhibited in the Hospital Carnival Procession, 1928.

This advertisement from the programme of The Lady Godiva procession and pageant on 29th June 1929 gives details of their new Edgwick Works, where they moved from their Butts premises. The vehicle and Turret Lathe indicated had taken part in the Hospital Carnival procession the previous year.

SPECIAL BROACHING MACHINE
For Broaching Crankshaft Bearings in position, made for Morris Motors Ltd., Engines Branch, Coventry

SPECIAL CONTINUOUS LOADING JIG
For Drilling Bolt Holes in Big End of Connecting Rods, made for Morris Motors Ltd., Engines Branch, Coventry

FINE TOOLMAKING

JIGS, TOOLING FIXTURES and PRESS TOOLS, MILLING CUTTERS of all types —including Inserted Teeth Cutters, HOBS, BROACHES, REAMERS. GAUGES of every kind including :

WICKMAN PATENT ADJUSTABLE LIMIT GAUGES
SPECIAL MACHINES & SPECIAL INSPECTION APPARATUS

Please send us your enquiries and write now for Catalogue

Coventry Gauge & Tool Co. (1928) Ltd., COVENTRY

Telephone—Coventry 3121 (3 lines)   Telegrams—" Gauges, Coventry."

Sole Makers of WICKMAN GAUGES, also Selling Agents

GLASGOW OFFICE—126, 126a BROOMIELAW

Telephone—Central 3219   Telegrams—" Autoplant, Glasgow."

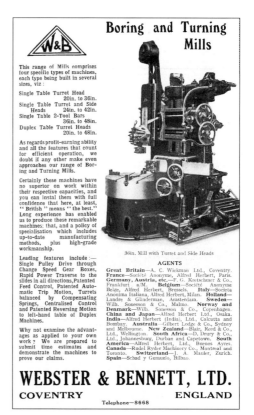

Boring and Turning Mills

This range of Mills comprises four specific types of machines, each type being built in several sizes, viz :

Single Table Turret Head
20in. to 36in.
Single Table Turret and Side Heads 24in. to 42in.
Single Table 2-Tool Bars
36in. to 48in.
Duplex Table Turret Heads
20in. to 48in.

As regards profit-earning ability and all the features that count for efficient operation, we doubt if any other make even approaches our range of Boring and Turning Mills.

Certainly these machines have no superior on work within their respective capacities, and you can instal them with full confidence that here, at least, " British " means " the best." Long experience has enabled us to produce these remarkable machines; that, and a policy of specialisation which includes up-to-date manufacturing methods, plus high-grade workmanship.

Leading features include :—
Single Pulley Drive through Change Speed Gear Boxes, Rapid Power Traverse to the slides in all directions, Patented Feed Control, Patented Automatic Trip Motion, Turrets balanced by Compensating Springs, Centralised Control and Patented Reversing Motion to left-hand table of Duplex Machines.

Why not examine the advantages as applied to your own work? We are prepared to submit time estimates and demonstrate the machines to prove our claims.

36in. Mill with Turret and Side Heads

AGENTS

Great Britain—A. C. Wickman Ltd., Coventry. France—Société Anonyme, Alfred Herbert, Paris. Germany, Austria, etc.—F. G. Kretschmer & Co., Frankfurt a/M. Belgium—Société Anonyme Belge, Alfred Herbert, Brussels. Italy—Societa Anonima Italiana, Alfred Herbert, Milan. Holland—Landre & Glinderman, Amsterdam. Sweden—Wilh. Sonesson & Co., Malmo. Norway and Denmark—Wilh. Sonesson & Co., Copenhagen. China and Japan—Alfred Herbert Ltd., Osaka. India—Alfred Herbert (India), Ltd., Calcutta and Bombay. Australia—Gilbert Lodge & Co., Sydney and Melbourne. New Zealand—Blair, Reed & Co., Ltd., Wellington. South Africa—D. Drury & Co., Ltd., Johannesburg, Durban and Capetown. South America—Alfred Herbert, Ltd., Buenos Ayres. Canada—Rudel Ryder Machinery Co., Montreal and Toronto. Switzerland—J. A. Mauler, Zurich. Spain—Schad y Gumuzio, Bilbao.

WEBSTER & BENNETT, LTD.

COVENTRY   ENGLAND

Telephone—8668

These two adverts taken from a City of Coventry official guide dated 1931 show typical machines being made by Coventry Gauge and Tool and Webster and Bennett. It is interesting that the loading jig and broaching machine in the left illustration were for Morris Motors Ltd, Engine Branch at that time still at the old Hotchkiss works in Gosford Street.

Coventry Gauge and Tool, Rover Road 1932 (Unknown)

Two years before this postcard the need to expand the original factory in Earlsdon had become desperate. Luckily at that time the Rover Company was transferring their organisation to Birmingham, which enabled part of the Meteor works in Queen Victoria Road to be utilised. The picture shows a railway horse and dray delivering goods to these premises. The number two and number three works indicated on the notice board were at that time manufacturing slip gauges and broaches.

Coventry Gauge and Tool Company Ltd, Fletchamstead Highway c1939 (Richards)

It was 26 years before this postcard that Harry Harley, the son of a watch maker and an ex Alfred Herbert apprentice, embarked on a small venture to manufacture jigs, tools and gauges, under the name of Walter Tatlow Ltd. The original premises, an old weaving mill in Earlsdon, together with additional premises acquired over the years were soon outgrown and it became essential to bring everything under one roof. In March 1936 Oscar Harmer of Alfred Herbert Ltd laid the foundation stone of the premises shown. At that time the Government announced re-armament plans and by 1939 the company, luckily, were fully geared up to meet the urgent war call for increased production.

A. C. WICKMAN LTD. COVENTRY

MACHINE TOOL SPECIALISTS

Branches at

LONDON ● BRISTOL ● BIRMINGHAM ● MANCHESTER ● GLASGOW

A.C Wickman Ltd, Rover Road 1938
A.C Wickman Ltd, Banner Lane 1939

Axel Wickman was a Swede who was trained at the Krupps works in Germany and came to this country in 1926 setting up his first small Charterhouse Works on the London Road. A year later he introduced Tungsten Carbide hardened steel tooling which considerably reduced tool wear and machine down time. Needing larger premises he moved into part of the Meteor Works on the corner of Rover Road and Queen Victoria Road, at that time being vacated by Rover. The top picture, an advert in the 1938 Hospital Carnival Programme shows these premises. After only three years he realised larger premises were needed and purchasing land at Banner Lane asked Hatterell & Partners to design a model factory for him. The 42,000 square feet building seen in the lower picture was build primarily for the manufacture of multi-spindle automatic lathes, the first in the world to embody automatic stroke-setting mechanisms. The premises were occupied in 1939 just in time to start making the machines that would mass-produce parts for the war effort.

ELECTRICAL

A less proclaimed though significant part of Coventry's industrial success has been its electrical industry. Two firms British Thompson Houston and General Electric Company have dominated this industry. Their early success was not linked to their later interests in electronic communication. None of the motor vehicles or aircraft made during the First World War could have functioned without a magneto to help them work. Most of the magnetos used in British industry were sourced from abroad (mainly Germany!), which made the industry very vulnerable at the outbreak of war. Fortunately BTH had been working on a suitable design and was ready to step into the breech. GEC in the guise of their subsidiary Connor Magneto Ignition built a factory on the site of the Copeswood Grange estate in 1916 and proceeded to add to the supply of magnetos. The BTH factory remained of great strategic importance in the Second World War as witness by the priority given to the factory by the Luftwaffe in their bombing raids. The inter-war years saw the development of the Copeswood site into the Peel-Connor Telephone Works whose extended factory opened in 1921. The development of telecommunications equipment continues at this factory today. BTH diversified into many different areas such as the development of loudspeakers, gramophones and film projectors. Today through various mergers both GEC and BTH are part of the same organisation.

Aerial View of Peel-Connor Telephone Works, Stoke c 1921 (Aerofilms)

Work on enlarging the original 1916 Connor Magneto Ignition Works had recently been completed when this photograph was taken. The factory was now in a position to capitalise on the booming telecommunications industry, but it already had a firm core of demand in the government contracts that it had won. Extensions were being added almost as soon as this original plant had been finished and by 1938 the factory was far bigger than that shown here, mainly making radio and telecommunications equipment.

A General View of the Works;
A Corner of the Dispatch Department;
c1921 (Unknown)

The way that manufacturers built houses for their workers is clearer at the Peel-Connor site than in most other Coventry factories. On the north side facing Binley Road and to the south (partly shown here at the end of Bourne Road), company houses were built to house the workers transferred from the old Salford factory in 1916. The second view shows the mainly female department where the smaller goods, particularly telecommunications parts, were dispatched. The male supervisor, Mr Smith, looks on. Even after the First World War Coventry was notable for the large proportion of female worker in its factories. Nevertheless, once married it was conventional in most factories for women to leave whether they wanted to or not.

PEEL-CONNER TELEPHONE WORKS
(Proprietors: The General Electric Co Ltd)
STOKE & COVENTRY
VIEWS of WORKS

A General View of the Works

Corner of Dispatch Dept.

Part of Final Inspection Dept.

Model Room

G.P.O. Inspection Room

Part of the Final Inspection Department;
Model Room;
GPO Inspection Room;
c1921 (Unknown)

These three views each show aspects of the factory's work from the earliest and the latest stages of the production process. The Model Room or Tool Room produces the press tools, jigs, gauges etc. which are needed for the construction of equipment. After assembly of manufactured and imported parts exchange apparatus and telephones have their final inspection. The GPO, who ran the British telephone service at the time, had their own team of inspectors in the factory to check the equipment they would be using. Thanks to its connections with Peel-Connor Coventry had the first automatic telephone exchange in the country installed in 1926.

Peel-Connor Telephone Works Hospital Carnival Float, Stoke 1926 (Appleby)

This works entry for the 1926 Hospital Carnival gives a useful illustration of the type of work done at the factory. The women cash collectors are all wearing dresses with pictures of radios with aerials on their heads. On one side of the float are nurses and patients listening to the radio while on the other is a large model of a RAF aeroplane. The works Maudslay lorry was connected up to a radio and blasted out programmes as it went.

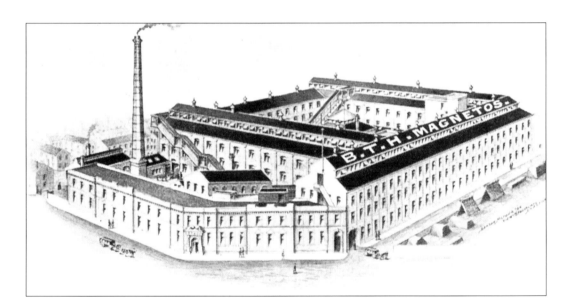

British Thompson-Houston Works, Lower Ford Street 1916

Not surprisingly manufacturers liked to show their premises in advertisements in the best possible light and until aerial photographs became more common an artistic impression was a good excuse to show an exaggerated version of reality. When BTH needed to expand from their base in Rugby they took over premises in the Stony Stanton Road in 1911/12, but soon they also needed more space and bought one of the vacant Humber factories in the city. The view shows this factory with Lower Ford Street to the left and All Saints Lane to the right. Part of the factory site remains today by Sky Blue Way.

Winding Department, BTH Works, Lower Ford Street, c1925

One thing that later wireless sets were not short of was wire. Wire coils were used in a number of BTH products from the loudspeaker that accompanied valve radio sets that were available from the mid 1920s to the motors and amplifiers used in the first electric gramophones. The development of loudspeakers instead of headphones saw the demand for the latter fall from 20,000 a week and the sale of the new radio speaker reaching a total of 250,000 units.

Making Wireless Headphones, BTH Works, Lower Ford Street, 1924 (Unknown)

Whilst plastics were a nineteenth century invention the version as 'Bakelite' was the one that found most common application after its invention in 1916. Amongst other things the insulating properties of the material meant it found a ready use in the fledgling electronics industry. BTH had their own moulding department where plastic parts were made for the radio headphones being assembled here.

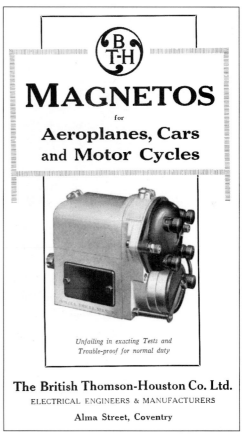

COAL MINING

It could be argued that coal mining is Coventry's oldest continuous industry, though the difficulty is one of definition of geographical area. Mining has gone on in the Coventry district at least since the middle ages, but it is only as the geographical boundaries of the city have grown in the last sixty years that they have come within the city's borders. It seems that such a fate has been like the kiss of death as one by one they have closed and with the recent closure of Coventry Colliery, Keresley there are none left. A large area beneath Coventry contains a broad coal seam. Permission to extract coal was given as early as the sixteenth century at Hawkesbury, Walsgrave and Wyken, but comprehensive extraction was far more common in the area north of Hawkesbury towards Nuneaton where the coal seam was at or near the surface. Despite the difficulties of accessing the coal, mining has had a more or less continuous history in the Coventry area since the late sixteenth century. A number of more modern pits were opened up through this well explored northern and eastern area during the late nineteenth and early twentieth centuries as well as developments at new locations in Binley and Keresley.

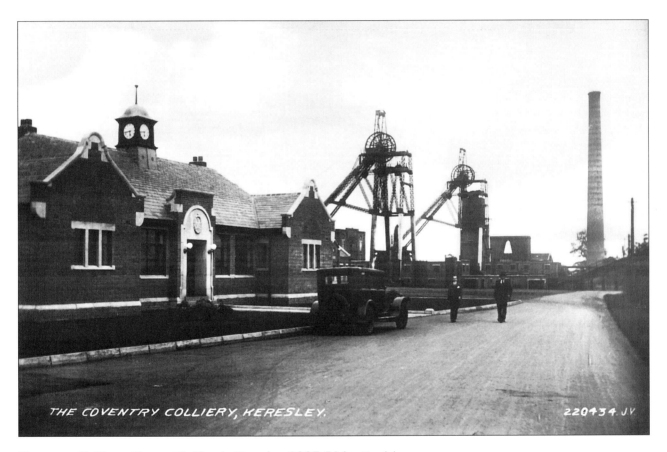

Coventry Colliery, Bennett's Road, Keresley 1927 (Valentine's)

In a number of ways the Coventry Colliery is an interesting pit. It was the last pit to be sunk in the Coventry area and when it opened in 1917 it was considered to have reserves that could last for at least a century. Sadly it lasted little more than seventy years. Its claim to be the first pit in Keresley is debatable as the Number One shaft, to the left in the picture, was in Exhall and the Number Two shaft just beyond it, was exactly on the Exhall-Keresley border. Some of the buildings such as the reception area in the foreground and the railway sidings, out of shot to the right were clearly in Keresley. On the surface this was the sort of model pit that many colliery companies could be proud of. This was as true of the immaculate way the grounds were kept on the colliery premises as it was for the upkeep of the colliery village and the facilities offered there. The status of Mr Fenn the colliery manager can easily be assessed by the size of his car and his home, Newland House built nearby.

The Colliery Boiler House, Keresley 1927 (Valentine's)

This internal view of the boiler house at Keresley Colliery gives an idea of the workings of the building shown on the following page at Binley Colliery. More reminiscent of a steamship than a coal mine this was a vital part of the functioning of a colliery as it provided the power for and lowering people and machinery via the pit head into the mine as well as bringing up the coal. It would also provide power for pumping out water, which was always a problem at Keresley, as well as helping ventilation.

Recreation Ground, Colliery Village, Keresley c1927 (Valentine's)

It is not easy to illustrate the way in which many industries were involved in many aspects of the workers lives other than providing work. Much of this was enlightened self-interest on the employers' behalf because without houses they would not attract enough workers. Factory social clubs were often used to help offset poor rates of pay. A colliery village was a complete example of an employer providing for most aspects of a workers life from work and accommodation to the aesthetic needs of music and play shown here by the creation of a park with bandstand. This was in keeping with Keresley being a model pit. The park even had a full time keeper. The park declined after nationalisation and the bandstand was taken down in 1971.

Craven Colliery, Henley Road, Wyken 1953 (M J Lee)

Today Henley Road crosses the centre of the picture from left to right and where the pump house chimney can be seen is the site of Henley Park Industrial estate. The clear area in the foreground, flanked by bushes, is the line of the old tramway that linked the Craven Colliery with the Alexandra Colliery a mile to the north. This still exists in part as the line of the Sowe Valley Way The colliery closed in 1907 and reopened in 1913 after a new shaft was sunk and new buildings erected, however it was to close again less than two decades later in 1927.

Binley Colliery, Willenhall Lane c1913 (Sylvester)

This rare view of Binley colliery shows the pit buildings three years after it opened. Already an extension to the boiler house appears to be in the process of being completed. In May 1907 Merry & Cunningham, a Glasgow firm had begun to open up the pit and in 1910 the first coal was brought to the surface. The estate to house the miners was started in 1909 and 60 buildings had been completed by 1913 along with a new school for the village. Eventually 300 houses were built to house at least some of the thousand or so miners, but at its closure in 1963 the pit was smallest in Warwickshire.

COVENTRY INDUSTRIAL EPHEMERA

As not all Coventry industrial concerns have represented themselves in postcard form, or even in readily accessible photographs, these two pages are an attempt to redress the balance of some of the major industries or companies not shown elsewhere.

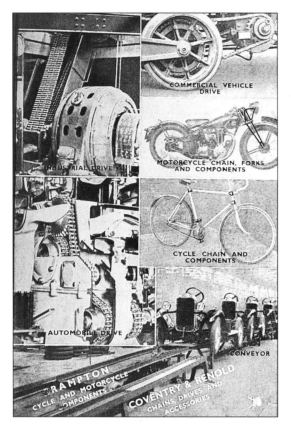

Brett's Stamping Co., Ltd.

MANUFACTURERS OF

STAMPINGS OR DROP FORGINGS

FOR THE **MOTOR**

CYCLE   AND GENERAL TRADES.

ENGINEERING

Harnall Lane, Coventry.

Telegrams BRETT'S, COVENTRY.
Telephone 168.

BRICO
TRADE MARK

PISTON RINGS

GUDGEON PINS

SHACKLE BOLTS

CENTRIFUGAL CASTINGS

GROUND CAST IRON BARS

Made in Coventry by

The British Piston Ring Co. Ltd.

Holbrook Lane
Coventry

Telephone—8014

H.P.

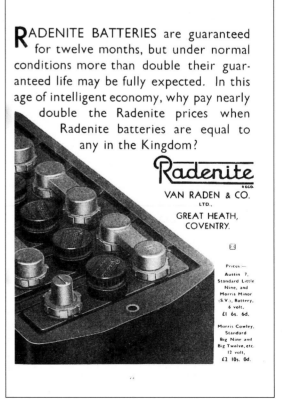

RADENITE BATTERIES are guaranteed for twelve months, but under normal conditions more than double their guaranteed life may be fully expected. In this age of intelligent economy, why pay nearly double the Radenite prices when Radenite batteries are equal to any in the Kingdom?

Radenite
REGD.

VAN RADEN & CO.
LTD.

GREAT HEATH,
COVENTRY.

Prices—
Austin 7,
Standard Little
Nine, and
Morris Minor
(S.V.), Battery,
6 volt,
£1 6s. 6d.

Morris Cowley,
Standard
Big Nine and
Big Twelve, etc.
12 volt,
£2 10s. 0d.

90

INDEX